Preface

Success in any competitive exam is as much about understanding the concepts as it is about mastering the art of problem-solving. One of the most effective strategies to achieve this mastery is through rigorous practice of previous years' question papers. This book is designed to provide you with a comprehensive collection of unsolved questions from past exams, serving as a critical tool in your preparation journey.

The questions included in this book of IGNOU Cyber and Cyber Laws Previous Years Unsolved Papers, are not just a reflection of what has been asked in the past, but they also represent the trends, patterns, and complexity levels that you are likely to encounter in future examinations. By working through these problems, you will not only strengthen your grasp of the subject matter but also enhance your ability to approach and solve different types of questions under exam conditions.

Each question in this book has been carefully selected to challenge your understanding and to push the boundaries of your knowledge. We believe that facing these challenges head-on, without immediately turning to solutions, fosters deeper learning and builds confidence. The goal is to encourage you to think critically, analyze problems from multiple angles, and develop a strategic approach to answering questions.While this book does not provide direct solutions, it is structured to support your learning process. You are encouraged to explore different methods of solving each problem, discuss with peers, and seek out resources that can guide you toward the correct answers. In doing so, you will not only prepare for your exams but also develop a stronger, more resilient mindset that is crucial for success in any competitive environment.

This collection is ideal for students at all levels—whether you are beginning your exam preparation, revising key concepts, or honing your problem-solving skills. As you work through these questions, remember that persistence and practice are your greatest allies. The more you engage with these problems, the more familiar you will become with the exam format, and the more confident you will be on the day of your test.In conclusion, this book is a companion designed to challenge, inspire, and ultimately, help you achieve your academic and professional goals. The path to success is rarely easy, but with dedication, hard work, and the right tools—such as this book—you are well on your way to mastering the material and excelling in your exams.

We wish you the best of luck in your preparation and hope that this book serves as a valuable resource on your journey to success.

Table of Contents

MCS-215

Master Of Computer Applications (MCA)
Chapter 1: Term-End Examination, December, 2021
Security And Cyber Laws

Time: 2 Hours
Maximum Marks: 50
Note: (i) Question No. 1 is compulsory.
(ii) Attempt any three questions from the rest

1. Explain the following in brief: $4 \times 5 = 20$
(a) The concept and need for cyber security
(b) Types of conventional ciphers
(c) Filtering devices and rating systems
(d) Difference between cybercrimes and traditional crimes

2. Discuss the core elements of data security. 10

3. Critically examine the copyright issues in digital medium. 10

4. Discuss the law in United States for regulation of cyberspace. 10

5. What is meant by Cryptography? Discuss RSA algorithm. 10

MCS-215

Master Of Computer Applications (MCA)
Chapter 2: Term-End Examination, June, 2022
Security And Cyber Laws

Time: 2 Hours
Maximum Marks: 50

Note: (i) Question No. 1 is compulsory.
(ii) Attempt any three questions from the rest

1. Explain the following in brief : 4x5=20
(a) Digital Signature
(b) Pros and Cons of Digital Security
(c) Cyber Security Threats
(d) UNCITRAL Model Law

2. Discuss the issues arising due to Linking, Inlining and Framing. 10

3. Discuss the conditions under which a person is liable to pay damages for violating the provisions of the Information Technology Act, 2000. 10

4. "Authentication is one of the most important of all information security objectives." Critically examine the statement. 10

5. Discuss in brief the various data security measures. 10

MCS-215

Master Of Computer Applications (MCA)
Chapter 3: Term-End Examination, December, 2022
Security And Cyber Laws

Time: 2 Hours
Maximum Marks: 50

Note: (i) Question No. 1 is compulsory.
(ii) Attempt any three questions from the rest

1. Explain the following in brief: 4x5=20
   (a) Data Management
   (b) Copyright and Related Rights
   (c) Advantages of Public Key Cryptography
   (d) Need for Regulation of Cyberspace

2. Discuss security issues in Cyberspace. 10

3. Write a note on Cyber Forensics. 10

4. Give an overview of Cyberspace regulation in India. 10

5. Discuss the six principles of Security Management. 10

MCS-215

Master Of Computer Applications (MCA)
Chapter 4: Term-End Examination, June, 2023
Security And Cyber Laws

Time: 2 Hours
Maximum Marks: 50

Note: (i) Question No. 1 is compulsory.
(ii) Attempt any three questions from the rest

1. (a) Explain any five security issues in cyberspace. 5
   (b) What are the three governing principles of data security? Explain how these three principles can be implemented. 6
   (c) Explain any two strategies of regulating the Internet. 4
   (d) What is the meaning of Intellectual Property? Explain the following forms of intellectual property: 5
      (i) Copyright and related rights
      (ii) Patents

2. (a) How can technology be used to answer the following security issues? 2+2+1
   (i) Unauthorized access
   (ii) Malwares
   (iii) Phishing

(b) What is the use of cryptography? Explain the concept of substitution cipher with the help of an example. 5

3. (a) Explain the concept and uses of digital signature and digital certificates. 5
   (b) Explain the following terms : 5
      (i) Security audit
      (ii) Security policy

2. (a) What is the purpose of using filtering devices and rating system on the Internet? Discuss the offences in the context of regulation of cyber law content in India. 5
(b) List the four categories of cyber crimes. List various cyber crimes of each category. How is cyber Crime different from traditional crime? 5

5. (a) What is cyber forensics? Explain with the help of an example. 5
   (b) What is Trademark? What are the different types of remedies available against infringement of trademark? 5

MCS-215

Master Of Computer Applications (MCA)
Chapter 5: Term-End Examination, December, 2023
Security And Cyber Laws

Time: 2 Hours
Maximum Marks: 50

Note: (i) Question No. 1 is compulsory.
(ii) Attempt any three questions from the rest

1. (a) What is a transposition cipher ? Explain with the help of an example. 5
(b) What is confidentiality and availability of data in the context of data security? Explain, how confidentiality can be maintained and availability can be ensured in a data management system. 5
(c) What are the liabilities of network service providers, in the context of cyber crimes? Explain. 5
(d) What are the possible trademark infringements related search engines? Explain. 5

2. Describe the following issues related to cyberspace: 10
(a) Distributed denial of service attack
(b) Malwares
(c) Crypto jacking
(d) Cyber physical attack
(e) Phishing

3. (a) What are the advantages and disadvantages of symmetric-key cryptography ? 5
(b) Explain the following security measures: 2+2+1
(i) E-mail security
(ii) Anti-virus protection
(iii) Access security

4. (a) What are the needs of regulating the cyberspace ? Explain. 5
(b) Explain the role of filtering devices and rating systems in the context of legal and self regulatory framework of cyberspace. 5

5. Explain the following terms in the context of cyber crimes and cyber laws and JPR issues : 10
(i) Cyber Forensics
(ii) Classification of cyber crimes
(iii) Domain name disputes
(iv) Framin

Chapter 6: Most Asked Questions Part-A

1. What are cyber laws and why are they important in the digital age?
Answer: Cyber laws refer to the legal regulations and frameworks that govern activities in the digital environment, including the internet, data privacy, and electronic transactions. They are essential in protecting individuals, organizations, and governments from cybercrimes such as hacking, identity theft, and data breaches. In the digital age, where sensitive information is shared online daily, cyber laws ensure accountability, regulate e-commerce, and safeguard digital rights. For MCA graduates, understanding cyber laws is crucial for building secure systems and ensuring compliance with legal standards to maintain user trust.

2. Explain the concept of cybersecurity and its significance in IT systems.
Answer: Cybersecurity involves the practice of protecting networks, systems, and data from unauthorized access, attacks, or damage. With the increasing reliance on digital platforms, cybersecurity ensures the confidentiality, integrity, and availability of information. It addresses threats like malware, phishing, and denial-of-service attacks. MCA graduates play a pivotal role in developing secure architectures, implementing firewalls, and regularly updating security protocols to protect sensitive information from cybercriminals and maintain organizational resilience.

3. Discuss the role of the Information Technology Act, 2000 in India's cyber legal framework.
Answer: The Information Technology (IT) Act, 2000 is India's primary legislation for governing digital activities. It provides legal recognition to electronic transactions and aims to address cybercrimes such as hacking, identity theft, and data breaches. The Act empowers authorities to investigate cyber offenses and prescribes penalties for violations. MCA graduates working in India must be familiar with the IT Act to design systems compliant with legal requirements and assist organizations in avoiding legal complications.

4. What are the major types of cybercrimes, and how can they be prevented?
Answer: Major types of cybercrimes include phishing, hacking, cyberstalking, identity theft, ransomware, and financial fraud. Prevention requires a combination of technical, legal, and educational measures. IT professionals can implement firewalls, antivirus software, and encryption to secure systems. MCA graduates should also promote user awareness about safe online practices and assist organizations in developing robust cybersecurity policies that comply with existing cyber laws.

5. Explain the concept of ethical hacking and its importance in cybersecurity.
Answer: Ethical hacking involves authorized attempts to identify vulnerabilities in systems and networks before malicious hackers exploit them. Ethical hackers, also called white-hat hackers, simulate attacks to strengthen security. For MCA graduates, learning ethical hacking techniques is crucial for building careers in cybersecurity. Ethical hacking protects sensitive data, supports compliance with regulations, and helps organizations proactively address security gaps.

6. Discuss the principles of data privacy and protection under cyber laws.
Answer: Data privacy ensures that individuals have control over how their personal information is collected, stored, and shared online. Cyber laws, like GDPR in Europe and India's Data Protection Bill, outline principles such as consent, data minimization, and the right to erasure. MCA graduates working with user data must understand these principles to develop systems that comply with privacy regulations and avoid legal or reputational risks for their organizations.

7. What is a digital signature, and how is it used in secure communication?
Answer: A digital signature is a cryptographic technique that authenticates the identity of the sender and ensures message integrity in electronic communication. It acts as a virtual fingerprint, preventing unauthorized alterations during transmission. In India, the IT Act recognizes digital signatures as legally valid. MCA graduates should understand how to implement digital signatures to enable secure transactions in banking, e-commerce, and government services.

8. Explain the role of firewalls in network security.
Answer: Firewalls act as barriers between internal networks and external threats by monitoring and controlling incoming and outgoing traffic based on predefined rules. They prevent unauthorized access, filter harmful content, and block suspicious activity. MCA graduates working in network administration must configure firewalls effectively and keep them updated to protect organizational assets from cyberattacks.

9. Discuss the legal implications of intellectual property rights (IPR) in cyberspace.
Answer: Intellectual Property Rights (IPR) in cyberspace protect digital assets such as software, multimedia content, and databases. Infringements like software piracy, copyright violations, and trademark misuse are punishable under cyber laws. MCA graduates should understand IPR to avoid violations in their work and educate clients about securing their digital creations legally.

10. What are the ethical and legal challenges of cloud computing under cyber laws?
Answer: Cloud computing raises ethical and legal issues around data privacy, cross-border data transfers, and responsibility for security breaches. Cyber laws often vary across jurisdictions, complicating compliance. MCA graduates developing cloud solutions must prioritize encryption, ensure transparency in data handling, and comply with international regulations like GDPR to mitigate risks and build user confidence.

11. Explain how encryption supports cybersecurity and legal compliance.
Answer: Encryption converts data into unreadable formats to prevent unauthorized access during storage or transmission. It protects sensitive information from hackers and supports compliance with privacy laws that mandate secure data handling. MCA graduates should learn encryption standards like AES and RSA to integrate security into software applications and ensure organizations meet legal obligations.

12. Discuss the role of cyber forensics in investigating cybercrimes.
Answer: Cyber forensics involves collecting, analyzing, and preserving digital evidence to investigate and prosecute cybercrimes. Techniques include recovering deleted files, tracing IP addresses, and analyzing malware. MCA graduates specializing in cybersecurity can contribute to forensic investigations by developing tools that assist law enforcement agencies in solving cyber offenses efficiently and within legal frameworks.

13. What is phishing, and how can organizations protect users against it?
Answer: Phishing is a cybercrime where attackers trick users into revealing sensitive information, such as passwords or financial details, via deceptive emails or websites. Organizations can protect users by implementing email filters, multi-factor authentication, and user education programs. MCA graduates must design systems with phishing detection mechanisms to minimize risks.

14. Explain cyber laws related to e-commerce and online transactions.
Answer: Cyber laws regulate e-commerce by addressing issues like consumer protection, digital contracts, taxation, and payment fraud. The IT Act in India validates electronic signatures and records, ensuring legal recognition of online transactions. MCA graduates must understand these laws to develop secure e-commerce platforms that comply with regulations and protect user rights.

15. Discuss the importance of cybersecurity awareness programs in organizations.
Answer: Cybersecurity awareness programs educate employees about safe online practices, reducing risks from human error such as weak passwords or clicking on phishing links. MCA graduates can design and deliver such programs to help organizations build a security-conscious culture. Awareness initiatives are vital for complying with legal obligations and preventing costly breaches.

16. Explain the legal aspects of data protection and privacy in India.
Answer: In India, data protection and privacy are governed by the IT Act, 2000 and the upcoming Personal Data Protection (PDP) Bill. These laws emphasize informed consent, purpose limitation, and accountability in data handling. Organizations collecting user data must ensure it is stored securely, used only for legitimate purposes, and shared with consent. MCA graduates working in IT must understand these legal provisions to design systems that comply with privacy standards and safeguard user trust while avoiding legal consequences.

17. What are the different types of malware, and how do they affect cybersecurity?
Answer: Malware refers to malicious software designed to disrupt, damage, or gain unauthorized access to systems. Common types include viruses, worms, trojans, ransomware, and spyware. These programs can steal data, encrypt files for ransom, or allow hackers to control devices remotely. MCA graduates should learn to identify and prevent malware by deploying antivirus software, intrusion detection systems, and educating users about safe practices. Preventing malware is critical for maintaining secure networks and meeting legal compliance requirements.

18. Discuss the importance of cyber ethics for IT professionals.
Answer: Cyber ethics refers to the responsible use of technology in a manner that respects privacy, intellectual property, and social norms. MCA graduates should adhere to ethical principles like honesty in coding, respecting confidentiality, and avoiding unauthorized access. Ethical practices prevent cybercrimes, ensure compliance with legal frameworks, and build public trust in IT professionals and their work. Cultivating strong ethical standards helps professionals navigate complex challenges in the evolving digital landscape.

19. Explain the role of VPNs in maintaining user privacy and security.
Answer: Virtual Private Networks (VPNs) create secure tunnels for internet traffic, encrypting data and masking user IP addresses. VPNs protect users from surveillance, hackers on public networks, and geo-restrictions. For MCA graduates, understanding VPN technology is essential for designing secure systems that comply with privacy laws and help organizations safeguard sensitive data during remote work scenarios.

20. What is cyberbullying, and how can laws help prevent it?
Answer: Cyberbullying involves using digital platforms to harass, threaten, or humiliate individuals. Victims often suffer psychological harm, prompting the need for legal protections. In India, sections of the IT Act and IPC (Indian Penal Code) criminalize online harassment. MCA graduates can contribute by developing reporting mechanisms, content filters, and awareness campaigns that support safer digital environments and ensure compliance with these legal provisions.

21. Discuss the significance of international treaties on cyber laws and security.
Answer: Cybercrimes often transcend borders, requiring international cooperation to address issues like hacking, terrorism, and data breaches. Treaties such as the Budapest Convention provide a framework for collaboration among countries. MCA graduates working in multinational organizations must understand these agreements to ensure their systems align with global cybersecurity standards and facilitate lawful cross-border data exchanges.

22. Explain the concept of cyber espionage and its legal implications.
Answer: Cyber espionage involves unauthorized access to confidential information, often targeting governments or corporations for strategic advantage. It is illegal under most national and international laws, as it threatens national security and business interests. MCA graduates in cybersecurity roles must design systems with strong encryption and intrusion detection to prevent espionage and ensure compliance with legal frameworks that penalize such acts.

23. What are honeypots in cybersecurity, and how are they used legally?
Answer: Honeypots are decoy systems designed to lure attackers, study their techniques, and protect real assets. Legally, organizations can deploy honeypots to strengthen security as long as they avoid violating user privacy or engaging in entrapment. MCA graduates can use honeypots ethically to gain insights into emerging threats and improve network defenses without infringing on cyber laws.

24. Discuss the challenges of enforcing cyber laws in the global digital space.
Answer: Enforcing cyber laws globally is challenging due to jurisdictional issues, differing legal standards, and anonymity on the internet. Cybercriminals exploit these gaps by operating from countries with weak regulations. MCA graduates must understand the complexities of international cyber law enforcement and design systems that comply with diverse legal frameworks, promoting collaboration between nations to combat global cyber threats effectively.

25. Explain how cyber laws address identity theft and fraud.
Answer: Identity theft involves stealing someone's personal information for fraudulent activities like financial scams

or fake accounts. Cyber laws criminalize such acts, prescribing penalties to deter offenders and protect victims. MCA graduates should implement multi-factor authentication, encryption, and monitoring tools to prevent identity theft and ensure systems meet legal standards for data protection.

26. What are the legal requirements for reporting data breaches under cyber laws?
Answer: Many countries, including India under its upcoming data protection framework, require organizations to report data breaches within specified timeframes. This includes notifying affected users and regulators to mitigate harm. MCA graduates managing IT systems must ensure organizations have breach response plans in place to comply with these reporting obligations and avoid legal penalties.

27. Discuss the role of digital evidence in prosecuting cybercrimes.
Answer: Digital evidence includes emails, logs, and files collected from electronic devices during cybercrime investigations. For admissibility in court, it must be authentic, reliable, and gathered legally using forensic tools. MCA graduates should understand the importance of preserving evidence integrity and designing systems that facilitate lawful collection while protecting user privacy.

28. Explain the concept of cyber extortion and measures to prevent it.
Answer: Cyber extortion involves threatening victims with data breaches, denial-of-service attacks, or ransomware unless a ransom is paid. Preventive measures include regular data backups, strong firewalls, and employee awareness training. MCA graduates in cybersecurity roles can design resilient systems and response strategies to combat extortion attempts effectively and reduce legal liabilities for organizations.

29. What are the implications of cyber terrorism under international law?
Answer: Cyber terrorism refers to using digital means to disrupt critical infrastructure, cause harm, or instill fear in populations. International laws treat such acts as severe crimes, necessitating collaboration among nations to counter threats. MCA graduates should understand the importance of securing critical systems like power grids and healthcare facilities against such attacks to ensure national security and compliance with global counter-terrorism initiatives.

30. Discuss how cyber insurance supports legal compliance in cybersecurity.
Answer: Cyber insurance provides financial protection against losses from cyber incidents like breaches or ransomware. It supports legal compliance by ensuring organizations can cover costs for regulatory fines, legal fees, and user notifications. MCA graduates should evaluate how cybersecurity policies integrate with cyber insurance plans to enhance organizational resilience and legal preparedness.

31. Explain the importance of secure coding practices in preventing cyber threats.
Answer: Secure coding practices involve writing software in a way that minimizes vulnerabilities such as SQL injection, buffer overflows, and cross-site scripting (XSS). These vulnerabilities can be exploited by attackers to gain unauthorized access or damage systems. MCA graduates should adopt practices like input validation, error handling, and code reviews to ensure robust applications. Secure coding aligns with legal requirements for protecting user data and helps organizations avoid breaches that could result in legal liabilities and reputational damage.

32. Discuss the role of multi-factor authentication (MFA) in enhancing cybersecurity.
Answer: Multi-factor authentication (MFA) adds an extra layer of security by requiring users to verify their identity using two or more methods, such as passwords, OTPs, or biometrics. MFA significantly reduces risks from stolen credentials and brute-force attacks. MCA graduates implementing MFA solutions help organizations comply with privacy regulations and enhance user trust by safeguarding sensitive data against unauthorized access.

33. What are cyber laws related to intellectual property protection in software development?
Answer: Cyber laws protect intellectual property (IP) in software through copyrights, patents, and trade secrets. Unauthorized copying, distribution, or modification of software is illegal and punishable under acts like the Indian Copyright Act and the IT Act. MCA graduates must understand these laws to ensure compliance when using third-party code and to protect their own creations from infringement.

34. Explain the role of digital forensics in securing organizational networks.
Answer: Digital forensics involves analyzing digital evidence to identify security breaches, trace attackers, and recover lost data. It supports investigations by preserving evidence integrity for legal proceedings. MCA graduates specializing in cybersecurity can assist in forensic investigations by designing systems that log activities accurately and allow quick incident response, helping organizations meet regulatory requirements.

35. Discuss the ethical implications of monitoring employee activity in workplaces.
Answer: Monitoring employee activity can improve productivity and security but raises ethical concerns about privacy and trust. MCA graduates developing such tools must ensure transparency by informing employees of monitoring practices and limit data collection to work-related activities. Ethical monitoring complies with privacy laws and fosters a respectful work environment while balancing organizational needs.

36. What are cyber laws regarding electronic contracts and signatures?
Answer: Cyber laws validate electronic contracts and digital signatures, ensuring their legal recognition. In India, the IT Act provides a framework for secure electronic transactions. MCA graduates must understand how to integrate digital signatures into systems securely, enabling organizations to conduct online business confidently while meeting legal standards for authenticity and non-repudiation.

37. Explain the significance of penetration testing in ensuring cybersecurity compliance.
Answer: Penetration testing involves simulating cyberattacks to identify vulnerabilities in networks, applications, or systems. It helps organizations strengthen defenses and comply with legal standards for data protection. MCA graduates skilled in penetration testing can assist companies in proactively addressing weaknesses and avoiding penalties for security breaches under cyber laws.

38. Discuss the legal implications of cyberstalking and harassment.
Answer: Cyberstalking and harassment involve using digital platforms to intimidate, threaten, or harm individuals. In India, these acts are punishable under the IT Act and IPC provisions. MCA graduates can develop reporting tools and monitoring mechanisms to help platforms detect and prevent such activities, ensuring compliance with laws and safeguarding user well-being.

39. What is ransomware, and how can organizations legally respond to such attacks?
Answer: Ransomware is malware that encrypts data and demands payment for its release. Legally, organizations are advised not to pay ransoms as it encourages cybercrime. Instead, they should report incidents to authorities, recover systems from backups, and strengthen security measures. MCA graduates can design resilient architectures and response plans that align with legal frameworks and reduce ransomware risks.

40. Explain the concept of cyber jurisdiction and its challenges in law enforcement.
Answer: Cyber jurisdiction determines which country's laws apply in digital disputes. Challenges arise because cybercrimes often cross borders, involving multiple jurisdictions. MCA graduates should design systems that comply with international standards and facilitate cooperation with global law enforcement agencies, helping organizations navigate complex legal environments effectively.

41. Discuss how cyber laws regulate online defamation.
Answer: Online defamation involves publishing false information that damages someone's reputation. The IT Act and IPC address online defamation in India, holding offenders accountable for defamatory posts, emails, or content. MCA graduates can implement content moderation tools and reporting mechanisms on platforms to help prevent defamation and ensure compliance with legal requirements.

42. Explain the role of CERT-In in India's cybersecurity framework.
Answer: The Indian Computer Emergency Response Team (CERT-In) coordinates responses to cybersecurity incidents, issues advisories, and assists organizations in strengthening defenses. MCA graduates should understand CERT-In's role in incident reporting and collaborate with it during cyberattacks to ensure compliance with national cybersecurity policies.

43. What are the legal provisions for protecting children online under cyber laws?
Answer: Laws like the IT Act include provisions to combat child pornography, cyberbullying, and exploitation. Globally, frameworks such as COPPA in the US set standards for protecting children online. MCA graduates must design child-safe platforms with parental controls and age verification to align with these legal requirements and promote a secure digital environment for minors.

44. Discuss how cyber laws address data localization requirements.
Answer: Data localization mandates that certain data be stored and processed within a country's borders to protect national security and privacy. In India, the RBI and PDP Bill advocate data localization for sensitive information. MCA graduates developing cloud solutions must ensure compliance with these regulations to avoid legal penalties and support secure data handling practices.

45. Explain the ethical challenges in designing AI-based surveillance systems.
Answer: AI surveillance systems can improve security but raise concerns about privacy, consent, and potential misuse. MCA graduates should implement ethical design principles by ensuring transparency, minimizing data collection, and incorporating safeguards against abuse. Balancing security with individual rights is essential for legal and societal acceptance of such technologies.

46. What is the role of encryption in complying with GDPR and similar privacy laws?
Answer: GDPR mandates organizations to protect user data through measures like encryption, ensuring confidentiality and integrity. MCA graduates must understand encryption protocols to implement systems that safeguard sensitive data and demonstrate compliance during audits, avoiding heavy penalties under privacy regulations.

47. Discuss how intellectual property theft impacts organizations and cyber law enforcement.
Answer: IP theft, such as stealing trade secrets or software code, harms innovation and causes financial losses. Cyber laws impose strict penalties for such offenses to deter criminals. MCA graduates should help organizations secure IP assets using access controls, monitoring systems, and awareness programs, ensuring protection against theft and legal compliance.

48. Explain the legal implications of financial frauds in cyberspace.
Answer: Financial frauds like phishing scams, credit card theft, and online payment frauds are punishable under cyber laws. Banks and e-commerce platforms must comply with regulatory standards to protect users. MCA graduates developing financial applications must integrate secure payment gateways and fraud detection systems to prevent such crimes.

49. What are the challenges of implementing cyber laws in developing countries?
Answer: Challenges include lack of awareness, weak enforcement mechanisms, and limited technical expertise. MCA graduates can contribute by developing affordable cybersecurity solutions, educating users, and assisting governments in building robust digital infrastructures to support effective cyber law enforcement.

50. Discuss the role of data anonymization in protecting user privacy under cyber laws.
Answer: Data anonymization removes personally identifiable information (PII) from datasets, ensuring user privacy while enabling data analytics. Many privacy laws mandate anonymization for compliance. MCA graduates should implement techniques like data masking and tokenization to protect user identities and avoid violations of legal and ethical standards.

51. Explain how cyber laws address issues related to social media misuse.
Answer: Social media misuse includes cyberbullying, fake news, identity theft, and defamation. Cyber laws like India's IT Act empower authorities to take action against such offenses, holding platforms and users accountable. MCA graduates working in this domain must develop mechanisms like content moderation, reporting tools, and privacy settings that align with legal requirements to ensure safe digital interactions.

52. Discuss the importance of cyber awareness training for employees in organizations.
Answer: Cyber awareness training educates employees on safe practices such as recognizing phishing attempts, using strong passwords, and reporting suspicious activities. This reduces human errors that often lead to breaches. MCA graduates can design training modules that align with industry regulations, fostering a security-conscious culture and helping organizations comply with legal standards for protecting data.

53. What are the legal implications of cross-border data transfers in cloud computing?
Answer: Cross-border data transfers involve moving user data between countries, raising concerns about privacy and compliance with varying laws. Frameworks like GDPR impose strict rules for such transfers. MCA graduates must design systems that encrypt data during transit, ensure legal agreements like Standard Contractual Clauses are in place, and support data localization where required.

54. Explain how cyber laws regulate online financial transactions to prevent fraud.
Answer: Cyber laws impose security requirements for online financial transactions to safeguard users from frauds like phishing or unauthorized charges. Provisions under the IT Act in India mandate secure payment systems and protect digital wallets. MCA graduates working on fintech solutions must integrate encryption and multi-factor authentication to ensure compliance with these regulations.

55. Discuss the ethical responsibilities of IT professionals in protecting user privacy online.
Answer: IT professionals have a moral obligation to ensure user data is collected, stored, and processed responsibly. MCA graduates must design systems with privacy-by-design principles, obtain informed consent, and provide users control over their data. Ethical handling of data aligns with legal requirements and fosters trust in digital services.

56. What are the challenges of enforcing cyber laws in combating fake news?
Answer: Fake news spreads rapidly, crossing jurisdictions and complicating enforcement. Legal challenges include identifying perpetrators while balancing freedom of speech. MCA graduates can design AI-based detection tools, promote user awareness, and help platforms comply with laws requiring content takedowns to curb misinformation responsibly.

57. Explain the role of cybersecurity audits in ensuring legal compliance.
Answer: Cybersecurity audits evaluate an organization's security posture against standards like ISO 27001 and regulatory frameworks. They identify vulnerabilities, assess compliance, and recommend improvements. MCA graduates can conduct or assist with audits, ensuring systems meet legal obligations and preventing penalties for non-compliance.

58. Discuss how cyber laws protect intellectual property in digital media.
Answer: Cyber laws like the Copyright Act safeguard intellectual property (IP) in digital formats, preventing unauthorized reproduction, distribution, or modification. MCA graduates working in creative industries must implement digital rights management (DRM) systems and monitor platforms for piracy to support IP protection.

59. What is the role of data breach notification laws in protecting consumers?
Answer: Data breach notification laws require organizations to inform regulators and affected users promptly after a breach. This transparency allows users to take preventive actions, like changing passwords or monitoring accounts. MCA graduates must ensure organizations have breach response plans that align with these legal requirements.

60. Explain the concept of cyber warfare and its legal implications.
Answer: Cyber warfare involves state-sponsored cyberattacks targeting another nation's infrastructure, often considered acts of aggression. International law lacks clear frameworks for cyber warfare, making attribution and accountability challenging. MCA graduates working in critical infrastructure must prioritize security to prevent such attacks and comply with emerging global regulations.

61. Discuss how cyber laws regulate online marketplaces to prevent fraud.
Answer: Online marketplaces must comply with cyber laws ensuring secure transactions, consumer rights protection, and grievance redressal mechanisms. The IT Act and Consumer Protection (E-commerce) Rules in India

govern these platforms. MCA graduates can design secure payment systems and user verification tools to enhance marketplace security and legal compliance.

62. What are the ethical implications of using artificial intelligence in cyber defense?
Answer: AI in cyber defense automates threat detection but raises ethical concerns like false positives and potential overreach into user privacy. MCA graduates should ensure transparency in AI systems, avoid biased algorithms, and include human oversight to maintain ethical standards while strengthening cybersecurity.

63. Explain how cyber laws address the challenges of online piracy.
Answer: Online piracy involves unauthorized sharing of copyrighted content like movies, music, and software. Cyber laws criminalize piracy and empower authorities to block infringing websites. MCA graduates working on digital platforms can integrate anti-piracy measures like watermarking and content monitoring to support compliance.

64. Discuss the role of digital literacy in reducing cybercrimes.
Answer: Digital literacy equips users with knowledge to recognize threats, practice safe online behavior, and report suspicious activities. MCA graduates can develop training programs and tools to promote cybersecurity awareness, complementing legal measures to reduce cybercrime effectively.

65. What are the legal provisions for addressing online hate speech?
Answer: Online hate speech is regulated under the IT Act and IPC in India, which criminalize content inciting violence or discrimination. MCA graduates working on content platforms must design AI-powered moderation systems and provide users reporting options to ensure compliance and maintain safe environments.

66. Explain the significance of cyber ethics in social media management.
Answer: Cyber ethics in social media involves promoting responsible communication, protecting user privacy, and avoiding manipulation. MCA graduates managing social media tools should prevent data misuse, ensure transparency in algorithms, and design platforms that discourage harmful content while aligning with ethical standards.

67. Discuss how cyber laws regulate access to sensitive government data.
Answer: Access to government data is tightly controlled under national security and privacy laws. Unauthorized access or leaks are punishable offenses. MCA graduates working in government IT systems must implement robust access controls, encryption, and monitoring to ensure compliance and safeguard critical data.

68. What are the ethical challenges in designing persuasive technologies for e-commerce?
Answer: Persuasive technologies in e-commerce can manipulate users into impulsive buying, raising ethical concerns. MCA graduates must design systems that respect user autonomy, provide clear disclosures about recommendations, and avoid exploitative tactics to ensure fairness and trust.

69. Explain the role of cyber laws in preventing online identity theft.
Answer: Cyber laws criminalize identity theft and mandate platforms to secure user data. MCA graduates can design systems with multi-factor authentication, encryption, and anomaly detection to protect user identities and comply with legal requirements.

70. Discuss the importance of ethical hacking certifications in legal cybersecurity practices.
Answer: Ethical hacking certifications, like CEH (Certified Ethical Hacker), validate professionals' skills in identifying vulnerabilities legally. MCA graduates pursuing these certifications can assist organizations in strengthening security while adhering to cyber laws that distinguish ethical testing from illegal hacking.

71. What are the challenges of implementing GDPR in global organizations?
Answer: GDPR's strict privacy rules pose challenges like adapting systems to comply, managing cross-border data transfers, and obtaining user consent. MCA graduates working in global firms must design systems with privacy by design principles and ensure compliance to avoid heavy penalties.

72. Explain how cyber laws address the spread of malware and cyberattacks.
Answer: Cyber laws penalize the creation, distribution, and use of malware. They also empower agencies to investigate and take down malicious networks. MCA graduates in cybersecurity roles should develop detection and prevention systems that support organizations in adhering to these legal standards.

73. Discuss the role of cyber security frameworks in supporting legal compliance.
Answer: Frameworks like NIST and ISO 27001 guide organizations in implementing security controls that align with legal obligations. MCA graduates can help organizations adopt these frameworks to manage risks effectively and demonstrate compliance during regulatory audits.

74. What are the ethical responsibilities of IT professionals in handling user consent?
Answer: IT professionals must ensure users provide informed consent for data collection and usage. MCA graduates should design clear consent mechanisms and allow users to manage their preferences, aligning with privacy laws and fostering ethical practices in digital systems.

75. Explain the legal and ethical considerations in using biometrics for authentication.
Answer: Biometrics offer secure authentication but raise privacy concerns due to the sensitivity of biometric data. Laws like GDPR mandate strict protection of such data. MCA graduates should implement encryption, allow alternative login options, and design systems that respect user privacy and comply with regulations.

76. Discuss how cyber laws address the issue of online radicalization and extremism.
Answer: Online radicalization involves using digital platforms to spread extremist ideologies and recruit individuals for unlawful activities. Cyber laws criminalize such actions and empower agencies to block content promoting violence or terrorism. MCA graduates working in security systems must design algorithms for detecting and reporting radical content while ensuring compliance with privacy and legal frameworks. Ethical considerations include balancing national security needs with the protection of freedom of speech.

77. Explain the legal provisions regarding spam emails and unsolicited communication.
Answer: Spam emails often include fraudulent schemes or malware distribution. Cyber laws, like India's IT Act and the CAN-SPAM Act in the US, prohibit sending bulk unsolicited messages without user consent. MCA graduates can integrate spam filters and opt-out mechanisms in systems to reduce spam and ensure compliance with regulations that protect users from digital harassment.

78. What is the significance of cyber law compliance in the healthcare sector?
Answer: Healthcare organizations store sensitive patient information, making them prime targets for cyberattacks. Laws like HIPAA in the US and India's PDP Bill require strict data protection practices. MCA graduates working in health IT must implement encryption, access controls, and secure communication protocols to protect data and comply with these legal standards, ensuring patient confidentiality and trust.

79. Discuss the ethical challenges of designing AI-powered surveillance drones.
Answer: Surveillance drones raise ethical concerns about privacy invasion, misuse by authorities, and unintended biases in tracking systems. MCA graduates must ensure clear policies for drone usage, secure data storage, and transparency in operations. Balancing security needs with citizens' rights is critical for creating ethically and legally compliant drone technologies.

80. Explain how cyber laws regulate online gaming platforms.
Answer: Online gaming platforms face issues like cyberbullying, addiction, and financial fraud. Cyber laws regulate these platforms by enforcing age restrictions, data privacy, and secure payment systems. MCA graduates working on gaming apps must integrate parental controls, content moderation tools, and secure authentication to align with these regulations and promote a safe gaming environment.

81. What are the legal implications of cyberattacks on critical infrastructure?
Answer: Cyberattacks on critical infrastructure like power grids, healthcare systems, or transportation networks are considered national security threats. International laws and national frameworks prescribe severe penalties for such

acts. MCA graduates designing such systems must prioritize cybersecurity measures like intrusion detection and ensure compliance with legal standards to prevent catastrophic consequences.

82. Discuss the ethical and legal challenges of biometric data collection in mobile applications.
Answer: Biometric data, such as fingerprints or facial scans, is highly sensitive and, if compromised, cannot be replaced. Laws like GDPR mandate explicit consent and strict protection of biometric data. MCA graduates developing mobile apps must use secure storage, provide alternative login options, and ensure ethical handling of such information to maintain user trust and legal compliance.

83. Explain how cyber laws address the issue of fake digital identities.
Answer: Fake digital identities are used for fraud, impersonation, and spreading misinformation. Cyber laws criminalize the creation and use of false identities online. MCA graduates can implement strong identity verification systems and anomaly detection mechanisms to prevent such abuses and ensure platforms remain secure and legally compliant.

84. What is cyber squatting, and how is it regulated under cyber laws?
Answer: Cyber squatting involves registering domain names similar to established brands with the intent to sell them at a profit or mislead users. Laws like the IT Act and international treaties such as ICANN's UDRP framework prohibit cyber squatting. MCA graduates managing web services must monitor domains to prevent misuse and assist in enforcing brand protection online.

85. Discuss the legal responsibilities of IT professionals in protecting confidential business data.
Answer: IT professionals have a legal obligation to secure business data against breaches and unauthorized access. Laws mandate the use of encryption, secure networks, and employee training to prevent insider threats. MCA graduates must design systems with strong access controls and ensure compliance with non-disclosure agreements (NDAs) and data protection regulations.

86. Explain the importance of ethical considerations in designing persuasive social media algorithms.
Answer: Social media algorithms shape user experiences and can influence opinions or behaviors. MCA graduates must avoid manipulative practices that exploit psychological vulnerabilities, ensuring algorithms are transparent and prioritize user well-being. Ethical design prevents addiction and aligns with privacy laws to maintain trust in social platforms.

87. What are the legal frameworks for addressing financial crimes in cyberspace?
Answer: Financial cybercrimes like phishing, online fraud, and money laundering are addressed by laws such as the IT Act, RBI guidelines in India, and international standards like FATF. MCA graduates developing financial technologies must integrate anti-fraud systems, comply with KYC (Know Your Customer) norms, and ensure secure transactions to prevent legal and financial risks.

88. Discuss how cyber laws address the sharing of explicit content online.
Answer: Sharing explicit content without consent, often termed revenge porn, is a criminal offense under cyber laws. The IT Act and POCSO Act in India impose strict penalties. MCA graduates working on platforms must implement robust content moderation tools and reporting mechanisms to detect and remove such material quickly, ensuring compliance and protecting users.

89. Explain how IT professionals can ensure compliance with data portability requirements under cyber laws.
Answer: Data portability allows users to transfer their data between service providers easily. Laws like GDPR mandate organizations to support this feature. MCA graduates should design systems with export functionalities that are secure and user-friendly, ensuring compliance and empowering users with control over their personal data.

90. What are the challenges of regulating the dark web under cyber laws?
Answer: The dark web facilitates illegal activities like drug trafficking, cybercrime, and weapon sales, often beyond the reach of traditional law enforcement. MCA graduates working in cybersecurity must develop advanced

monitoring tools and collaborate with global agencies to trace criminal networks while ensuring their methods comply with privacy and surveillance laws.

91. Discuss how cyber laws address the issue of deepfake technology misuse.
Answer: Deepfakes can spread misinformation, harm reputations, and manipulate public opinion. Cyber laws criminalize the malicious use of such content. MCA graduates can design detection tools and reporting systems to identify and mitigate deepfake threats, supporting platforms in maintaining compliance and user safety.

92. Explain the role of incident response teams in legal compliance.
Answer: Incident response teams (IRTs) handle cybersecurity breaches by containing threats, recovering data, and reporting incidents to regulators as required by law. MCA graduates can contribute by developing response strategies and ensuring teams are trained to meet deadlines for breach notifications, avoiding penalties and reputational damage.

93. What is the role of digital signatures in e-governance under cyber laws?
Answer: Digital signatures authenticate users and ensure data integrity in e-governance systems. Recognized legally under the IT Act, they enable secure online services like tax filings and license renewals. MCA graduates should integrate digital signature functionalities to support seamless and compliant e-governance solutions.

94. Discuss the ethical implications of AI systems in cybersecurity surveillance.
Answer: AI in surveillance automates threat detection but raises concerns about overreach, privacy violations, and false positives. MCA graduates must design systems with clear accountability, human oversight, and transparency to ensure ethical use and compliance with privacy laws.

95. Explain how cyber laws regulate the use of encryption technologies.
Answer: While encryption secures data, governments often regulate its use to prevent misuse by criminals. In India, the IT Act allows encryption but imposes limits on key lengths for certain sectors. MCA graduates must design systems that comply with these regulations while ensuring user data remains secure.

96. What are the ethical challenges of using predictive analytics for employee monitoring?
Answer: Predictive analytics in monitoring may lead to employee stress, privacy violations, or biased evaluations. MCA graduates should ensure transparency, obtain consent, and use such tools to support rather than penalize employees. Ethical implementation maintains workplace trust and aligns with labor laws.

97. Discuss how cyber laws address hacking and unauthorized system access.
Answer: Hacking and unauthorized access are criminalized under the IT Act, which prescribes penalties including imprisonment. MCA graduates in cybersecurity roles must implement intrusion detection systems and secure authentication methods to protect systems and comply with these legal requirements.

98. Explain how cyber laws regulate the sale of counterfeit products online.
Answer: Online marketplaces are held accountable under cyber laws for listing counterfeit goods. Regulations require platforms to verify sellers and remove infringing items promptly. MCA graduates working on such platforms can integrate AI-based product verification systems to ensure compliance and protect consumers.

99. What are the legal responsibilities of IT professionals in ensuring accessibility in digital platforms?
Answer: Accessibility laws mandate that digital platforms cater to users with disabilities. MCA graduates must design websites and apps that comply with standards like WCAG (Web Content Accessibility Guidelines) to avoid discrimination and ensure inclusivity, meeting both ethical and legal obligations.

100. Discuss the significance of ethical hacking in supporting law enforcement agencies.
Answer: Ethical hackers assist law enforcement by identifying system vulnerabilities and simulating attacks to improve defenses. MCA graduates can collaborate with agencies to investigate cybercrimes legally, ensuring their activities remain within the scope of ethical guidelines and cyber laws.

101. Explain the role of cyber laws in addressing online financial scams and phishing attacks.
Answer: Cyber laws criminalize phishing, where attackers deceive users into revealing confidential data like passwords or financial details. Laws like India's IT Act empower authorities to prosecute perpetrators and mandate organizations to secure their systems. MCA graduates can integrate phishing detection tools, educate users, and ensure platforms comply with these regulations to minimize scams and financial fraud online.

102. Discuss how cyber laws regulate electronic payment systems.
Answer: Electronic payment systems must follow cybersecurity guidelines to ensure secure transactions. Laws such as RBI regulations in India mandate secure authentication and encryption protocols. MCA graduates designing fintech applications must ensure PCI-DSS compliance and integrate robust fraud detection mechanisms to align with these legal frameworks.

103. What are the ethical responsibilities of IT professionals in ensuring cybersecurity for e-commerce platforms?
Answer: IT professionals must safeguard customer data, ensure secure transactions, and prevent breaches on e-commerce platforms. MCA graduates should implement SSL certificates, data encryption, and regular vulnerability testing. Ethical practices promote user trust and help organizations comply with cyber laws, protecting them from legal penalties and reputational damage.

104. Explain how cyber laws address the issue of child exploitation online.
Answer: Child exploitation, including sharing obscene content and cyberbullying, is strictly prohibited under the IT Act and POCSO Act in India. Global frameworks like COPPA in the US provide additional protection. MCA graduates working on digital platforms should integrate age verification, content filters, and reporting mechanisms to prevent such offenses and support legal enforcement.

105. Discuss the importance of privacy policies in compliance with cyber laws.
Answer: Privacy policies inform users about how their data is collected, stored, and shared. Laws like GDPR require organizations to provide clear and concise privacy notices. MCA graduates must design systems that enforce these policies, ensuring user consent and helping organizations avoid legal disputes over data handling practices.

106. What are the legal consequences of unauthorized access to government systems?
Answer: Unauthorized access to government systems is considered a serious offense under cyber laws and may result in imprisonment and heavy fines. MCA graduates managing such systems must implement stringent access controls, multi-factor authentication, and regular audits to prevent breaches and ensure compliance with legal frameworks.

107. Explain the ethical considerations in developing tracking technologies for mobile applications.
Answer: Tracking technologies, such as GPS-based features, raise privacy concerns if misused. MCA graduates must ensure transparency in data collection, seek user consent, and provide options to disable tracking. Ethical practices align with privacy laws and prevent potential misuse of sensitive location data.

108. Discuss how cyber laws regulate content moderation on social media platforms.
Answer: Social media platforms are legally obligated to moderate content that violates laws, including hate speech, misinformation, or explicit material. The IT Rules in India outline intermediary responsibilities. MCA graduates working on moderation tools should ensure compliance while balancing freedom of expression and ethical considerations.

109. What are the legal implications of distributing pirated software online?
Answer: Distributing pirated software violates copyright laws and attracts penalties, including fines and imprisonment. MCA graduates must educate users about licensed software, integrate anti-piracy protections, and ensure compliance with cyber laws to support intellectual property rights.

110. Explain the significance of ethical practices in handling user data breaches.
Answer: Ethical practices in handling breaches involve promptly notifying affected users, mitigating harm, and

reporting incidents to regulatory authorities. MCA graduates should develop incident response plans that align with laws like GDPR's 72-hour breach notification requirement, ensuring accountability and maintaining user trust.

111. Discuss the challenges of regulating cryptocurrencies under cyber laws.
Answer: Cryptocurrencies pose challenges like anonymous transactions, money laundering, and fraud. Many countries are still developing regulatory frameworks to govern crypto activities. MCA graduates working in blockchain and fintech must stay updated on evolving laws and design systems that support compliance, including KYC/AML requirements.

112. Explain how cyber laws address the issue of revenge porn and online harassment.
Answer: Revenge porn and harassment are criminal offenses under the IT Act and IPC in India. MCA graduates should integrate AI-based content detection and reporting features in platforms to assist authorities in taking swift action against offenders and supporting victims.

113. What is the importance of cybersecurity certifications for legal compliance?
Answer: Certifications like ISO 27001 and PCI-DSS validate an organization's adherence to security standards and legal requirements. MCA graduates pursuing certifications like CEH or CISSP can help organizations implement best practices, ensuring systems are robust and compliant with cyber laws.

114. Discuss how cyber laws regulate the use of artificial intelligence in decision-making systems.
Answer: AI in decision-making raises concerns about bias, accountability, and data privacy. Cyber laws require transparency and fairness in automated systems. MCA graduates developing AI tools must ensure explainability, avoid discriminatory outcomes, and comply with data protection laws to mitigate legal risks.

115. Explain the legal responsibilities of IT professionals in protecting intellectual property rights.
Answer: IT professionals must prevent unauthorized use or sharing of copyrighted software, designs, and content. MCA graduates should enforce licensing agreements, use proper attribution for open-source components, and ensure compliance with intellectual property laws to safeguard organizational and client assets.

116. What are the ethical challenges of AI-powered facial recognition systems?
Answer: Facial recognition raises concerns about surveillance, consent, and potential misuse. MCA graduates must design systems with clear user opt-ins, avoid biases, and comply with privacy laws to balance technological benefits with ethical responsibilities.

117. Discuss the significance of legal frameworks for cybersecurity in critical sectors like banking.
Answer: Banking systems handle sensitive financial data, making them prime targets for cyberattacks. Laws like RBI's cybersecurity guidelines in India mandate strict security controls. MCA graduates working in fintech must ensure systems comply with these frameworks to protect user data and maintain financial stability.

118. Explain how cyber laws regulate cross-border online defamation cases.
Answer: Online defamation often involves multiple jurisdictions, complicating enforcement. International treaties and mutual legal assistance agreements (MLATs) facilitate cooperation between countries. MCA graduates working on global platforms should design content reporting and takedown mechanisms that comply with diverse legal standards.

119. What are the ethical considerations in deploying predictive policing technologies?
Answer: Predictive policing risks reinforcing biases and infringing on civil liberties. MCA graduates must design systems with fairness audits, human oversight, and transparency to ensure ethical use while complying with privacy and cyber laws.

120. Discuss the legal provisions for protecting consumer rights in e-commerce.
Answer: Laws like the Consumer Protection (E-Commerce) Rules in India regulate unfair trade practices, return policies, and secure payments. MCA graduates must design platforms that ensure compliance by offering user-friendly policies and safeguarding transaction data.

121. Explain the importance of digital forensics in cyber law enforcement.
Answer: Digital forensics helps investigate cybercrimes by recovering evidence from devices and networks. MCA graduates can assist by designing systems with proper logging and evidence preservation mechanisms that support legal investigations and prosecutions.

122. Discuss how cyber laws regulate the ethical use of drones in civilian areas.
Answer: Drone usage is regulated to prevent privacy violations, accidents, and security risks. In India, DGCA guidelines mandate permissions for certain operations. MCA graduates developing drone software must ensure compliance with these laws to enable safe and ethical deployment.

123. What are the legal implications of using fake profiles on networking platforms?
Answer: Creating fake profiles is a violation of cyber laws and may result in penalties under the IT Act. MCA graduates working on networking platforms should design robust verification systems to detect and prevent impersonation.

124. Explain how cyber laws address cyber terrorism threats.
Answer: Cyber terrorism involves using digital means to disrupt critical systems and incite fear. Laws impose strict penalties for such acts and mandate cybersecurity for critical infrastructure. MCA graduates must design resilient systems that align with national security policies to counter these threats effectively.

125. Discuss the significance of cyber security awareness in legal compliance.
Answer: Security awareness helps employees recognize threats like phishing and follow safe practices, reducing legal risks. MCA graduates can design awareness programs that align with laws requiring organizations to demonstrate proactive security measures, ensuring compliance and protecting user data.

126. Discuss how IT professionals should ethically manage user profiling in targeted e-commerce marketing.
Answer: User profiling helps e-commerce platforms recommend products but raises privacy concerns if data is collected without consent. MCA graduates must design systems that obtain explicit user permission, anonymize sensitive data, and provide clear privacy policies. Ethical practices include giving users control over data sharing preferences and ensuring compliance with laws like GDPR to prevent misuse or manipulative targeting.

127. Explain the ethical responsibilities of IT professionals in managing digital rights management (DRM) systems for creative content.
Answer: DRM systems protect intellectual property but can restrict legitimate user access. MCA graduates must design DRM tools that balance content creator rights with user freedoms, ensuring fair usage policies and preventing overreach. Ethical practices involve complying with copyright laws while maintaining accessibility for users who have lawfully purchased content.

128. Evaluate how IT professionals can prevent misuse of personal data in facial recognition systems used in airports.
Answer: Facial recognition systems enhance airport security but risk data breaches and privacy violations. MCA graduates should implement encryption, limit data retention, and ensure transparency about how data is collected and used. Ethical practices include obtaining informed consent and complying with aviation and privacy laws to protect passengers' rights.

129. Discuss the legal and ethical implications of cyberattacks on educational platforms delivering online exams.
Answer: Cyberattacks on online exam platforms compromise fairness and data security. MCA graduates must develop secure authentication methods, encryption protocols, and real-time monitoring systems to prevent breaches. Ethical responsibilities involve ensuring student privacy, complying with data protection laws, and providing mechanisms to report suspicious activity.

130. Explain how IT professionals can ethically handle the collection of user behavior data for UI/UX improvements.

Answer: Collecting user behavior data helps improve user experience but can be intrusive if done without consent. MCA graduates should anonymize data, obtain explicit user permission, and comply with privacy laws. Ethical practices include allowing users to opt out of tracking and being transparent about how their data contributes to UI/UX development.

131. Analyze the ethical challenges of deploying AI-based surveillance systems in workplaces.
Answer: AI surveillance systems may improve security but can also violate employee privacy and autonomy. MCA graduates should ensure transparency, limit surveillance to work-related contexts, and avoid misuse for micromanagement. Ethical practices align with labor laws and promote a healthy work environment while safeguarding organizational interests.

132. Discuss how cyber laws regulate the use of artificial intelligence in autonomous delivery robots.
Answer: Autonomous delivery robots operate in public spaces and must comply with safety and privacy laws. MCA graduates developing these systems should integrate obstacle detection, data encryption, and clear user notifications. Ethical practices involve minimizing surveillance and ensuring accountability in case of malfunctions or accidents.

133. Explain how IT professionals can ethically manage user-generated data in health and fitness communities.
Answer: Health and fitness communities often involve sharing sensitive personal data. MCA graduates must design secure systems with privacy settings, consent mechanisms, and moderation tools to prevent misuse. Ethical practices include compliance with health data protection laws and respecting user choices about data visibility.

134. Evaluate the legal implications of cross-border cyber espionage activities.
Answer: Cross-border cyber espionage violates international laws and threatens national security. MCA graduates in cybersecurity roles must design systems with intrusion detection, secure communication channels, and compliance with global treaties like the Budapest Convention to deter such activities. Ethical practices involve cooperating with authorities to report incidents while protecting sensitive organizational data.

135. Discuss how IT professionals should handle ethical dilemmas in developing persuasive notifications in mobile apps.
Answer: Persuasive notifications can engage users but may encourage overuse or addiction. MCA graduates should design notifications that prioritize user well-being, such as reminders for breaks or healthy usage. Ethical practices align with digital wellness principles and avoid manipulative techniques that exploit psychological vulnerabilities.

136. Explain how cyber laws regulate online auction platforms to prevent fraud.
Answer: Online auction platforms are vulnerable to scams like fake bids and payment fraud. Cyber laws require these platforms to implement verification systems, secure payment gateways, and user protection policies. MCA graduates must design fraud detection mechanisms and ensure compliance with e-commerce regulations to build user trust.

137. Analyze the ethical considerations of deploying AI-powered hiring chatbots for large organizations.
Answer: Hiring chatbots automate recruitment but risk bias and lack of transparency in shortlisting candidates. MCA graduates should ensure fairness, train AI on diverse datasets, and provide candidates with appeal mechanisms. Ethical practices comply with employment laws and promote inclusivity in hiring processes.

138. Discuss how IT professionals can ethically manage data analytics in personalized education platforms.
Answer: Personalized learning platforms analyze student data to tailor content but may risk profiling and data breaches. MCA graduates should anonymize data, secure storage systems, and provide students with control over what data is shared. Ethical practices involve complying with education privacy laws and designing systems that support equitable learning opportunities.

139. Explain the legal and ethical responsibilities of IT professionals in designing online grievance redressal systems.
Answer: Grievance systems must ensure confidentiality and protect user identities. MCA graduates should design

secure submission portals, encryption for sensitive data, and tracking mechanisms for complaints. Ethical practices align with cyber laws and ensure fair resolution processes that foster user trust in digital platforms.

140. Evaluate how IT professionals can ensure ethical deployment of AI in autonomous drones for delivery services.

Answer: Autonomous drones face ethical challenges like privacy invasion and safety risks. MCA graduates should design drones with geofencing, obstacle avoidance, and limited data collection. Compliance with aviation laws and transparency about operational practices ensure ethical and responsible deployment.

141. Discuss the ethical challenges of using AI chatbots in customer service for mental health support.

Answer: AI chatbots assist users in mental health services but lack empathy and nuanced understanding. MCA graduates must design systems that clearly inform users of limitations, involve professionals for critical cases, and comply with health privacy laws. Ethical deployment ensures AI supports human services rather than replacing them entirely.

142. Explain how cyber laws address unauthorized access to social media accounts.

Answer: Unauthorized access to accounts constitutes hacking and is punishable under the IT Act and global cybercrime frameworks. MCA graduates must design systems with multi-factor authentication, anomaly detection, and user notification features to prevent such breaches and ensure compliance with legal standards.

143. Analyze how IT professionals can ethically handle requests for user surveillance data from private organizations.

Answer: Requests for surveillance data must adhere to privacy laws and require user consent or legal authorization. MCA graduates should verify such requests, provide only minimal necessary data, and advocate for transparency to prevent misuse. Ethical practices involve protecting user rights while balancing organizational needs.

144. Discuss how IT professionals can promote ethical practices in data monetization strategies.

Answer: Data monetization generates revenue but can exploit users if not handled transparently. MCA graduates should design systems that anonymize data, inform users of monetization practices, and offer opt-out options. Ethical practices align with data protection laws and prioritize user trust over profit.

145. Explain the role of IT professionals in implementing cybersecurity frameworks for small businesses.

Answer: Small businesses often lack robust security, making them targets for cyberattacks. MCA graduates should implement affordable cybersecurity solutions like firewalls, backups, and employee training. Ethical practices involve educating owners about threats and complying with regulations to protect customer data and business continuity.

Chapter 7: Most Asked Questions Part-B

1. Analyze a situation where an organization faces a ransomware attack. What ethical and legal steps should IT professionals take?
Answer: When an organization experiences a ransomware attack, IT professionals must act ethically by prioritizing user data protection and ensuring compliance with cyber laws. The first step is to isolate infected systems to prevent further spread. Legal requirements often mandate notifying authorities like CERT-In in India within a stipulated timeframe. Ethical practices include informing affected stakeholders, avoiding payment of ransom to discourage cybercriminals, and recovering data from secure backups. MCA graduates must design and implement response strategies, ensuring adherence to privacy laws and minimizing operational and reputational damage.

2. Discuss how IT professionals should handle cross-border data transfer requests from international clients.
Answer: Cross-border data transfer involves sharing data between countries, which can raise legal challenges due to varying privacy laws like GDPR in Europe. IT professionals must assess whether the destination country offers adequate data protection. MCA graduates should ensure data is encrypted during transmission, obtain informed consent from users, and include contractual clauses for compliance. Ethical practices involve transparency with clients and users about where and how their data is stored, balancing global collaboration with legal obligations.

3. Evaluate the ethical challenges faced while designing surveillance systems for public spaces.
Answer: Surveillance systems enhance public safety but raise concerns about privacy, consent, and potential misuse by authorities. MCA graduates must design systems with safeguards like data minimization, access controls, and transparency in usage policies. Ethical challenges include preventing bias in AI facial recognition and ensuring citizens are informed about monitoring practices. Balancing security with individual rights is crucial to comply with privacy laws and avoid creating a surveillance-heavy society.

4. Explain the legal and ethical considerations of hosting user-generated content platforms.
Answer: Platforms like social media face challenges with user-generated content, including hate speech, misinformation, and copyright violations. Cyber laws hold platforms liable if they fail to moderate harmful content. MCA graduates developing such systems must integrate content filtering tools, reporting mechanisms, and comply with IT intermediary rules. Ethical considerations involve balancing freedom of speech with responsibility to prevent harm, ensuring transparency in moderation policies, and protecting user privacy.

5. Discuss how IT professionals should ethically manage employee monitoring in remote work environments.
Answer: Remote work monitoring tools help track productivity but raise privacy concerns. MCA graduates must design systems that are transparent, informing employees about the type and purpose of monitoring. Ethical practices include limiting monitoring to work-related activities, anonymizing sensitive data, and complying with privacy laws like India's IT Rules or GDPR. Balancing organizational needs with respect for employee autonomy fosters trust and legal compliance.

6. Analyze the ethical implications of deploying AI-based predictive policing tools.
Answer: Predictive policing tools aim to forecast crime hotspots but risk reinforcing societal biases if trained on skewed data. MCA graduates working on such systems must ensure fairness audits, engage diverse stakeholders in development, and provide transparency in algorithmic decisions. Ethical deployment requires human oversight to avoid misuse and compliance with legal standards that protect civil liberties and prevent discriminatory outcomes.

7. Discuss how IT professionals should handle a situation where their organization's software is used unethically by third parties.
Answer: If software is misused, IT professionals have a duty to investigate and report to management. MCA graduates should recommend technical safeguards like usage restrictions and terms of service enforcement to limit unethical applications. Ethical practices involve engaging legal teams to address misuse, alerting authorities if laws are violated, and updating software policies to prevent recurrence while maintaining organizational integrity.

8. Evaluate the legal implications of using unlicensed software in organizations.
Answer: Using unlicensed software violates intellectual property laws and exposes organizations to lawsuits, fines,

and reputational harm. MCA graduates should advocate for the use of licensed or open-source alternatives, conduct software audits, and educate staff about the risks. Ensuring compliance not only avoids legal penalties but also supports ethical business practices that respect creators' rights.

9. Explain how IT professionals can address ethical issues in developing addictive mobile applications.
Answer: Mobile apps designed for high user engagement can become addictive, leading to health and productivity issues. MCA graduates must design features like usage reminders, parental controls, and screen-time limits to promote healthy interaction. Ethical design aligns with legal frameworks regulating user well-being, ensuring apps support positive behavior without exploiting psychological vulnerabilities.

10. Discuss how IT professionals should manage data privacy when designing IoT devices for homes.
Answer: IoT devices in homes collect sensitive personal data, making privacy paramount. MCA graduates must implement encryption, secure user consent mechanisms, and provide clear data usage disclosures. Ethical practices involve giving users control over what data is collected and shared, ensuring compliance with privacy laws such as GDPR or India's PDP Bill to avoid potential misuse or breaches.

11. Analyze the ethical responsibilities of IT consultants advising clients on cybersecurity investments.
Answer: IT consultants must prioritize client interests, offering unbiased advice that meets legal and organizational needs. MCA graduates should avoid recommending unnecessary or overpriced solutions for personal gain. Ethical consultancy involves transparent communication, staying updated on cyber laws, and ensuring that recommended measures align with regulatory requirements to protect both client data and reputation.

12. Discuss how IT professionals can balance innovation with ethical concerns in AI healthcare systems.
Answer: AI in healthcare enhances diagnosis and treatment but raises ethical concerns about data privacy, bias, and accountability. MCA graduates must design systems with secure data handling, transparent algorithms, and oversight from medical professionals. Ethical AI supports patient safety, complies with health data laws like HIPAA or PDP, and complements rather than replaces human expertise.

13. Explain how IT professionals should approach whistleblowing in cases of organizational cybersecurity violations.
Answer: Whistleblowing is critical when organizations engage in illegal or unethical cybersecurity practices. MCA graduates should first report concerns internally through secure channels. If ignored and public interest is at stake, legal whistleblower protections may justify external reporting. Ethical whistleblowing prioritizes transparency and accountability while minimizing harm to stakeholders.

14. Discuss the role of ethical hacking in supporting government cyber defense initiatives.
Answer: Ethical hackers test systems for vulnerabilities, helping governments prevent cyberattacks. MCA graduates working in this field must operate within legal boundaries, obtain necessary permissions, and ensure sensitive data is handled securely. Ethical hacking strengthens national cybersecurity and supports compliance with laws protecting critical infrastructure.

15. Analyze the ethical considerations of deploying surveillance apps during a public health crisis.
Answer: During crises like pandemics, surveillance apps track infections but may compromise privacy. MCA graduates developing such apps must ensure transparency, obtain user consent, and limit data collection to health-related purposes. Ethical practices involve balancing public safety with individual rights and complying with data protection laws to avoid misuse post-crisis.

16. Evaluate the legal and ethical considerations of using biometric authentication in banking apps.
Answer: Biometric authentication enhances security in banking apps but raises concerns about the storage and protection of sensitive data. Laws like GDPR and India's Data Protection Bill require explicit consent and robust encryption of biometric information. MCA graduates must ensure alternative authentication options for users uncomfortable with biometrics. Ethical practices include transparent policies, securing biometric templates, and ensuring users understand how their data will be used and stored to prevent misuse.

17. Discuss how IT professionals should handle the ethical dilemma of being asked to create spyware for an organization.
Answer: Developing spyware to secretly monitor users violates privacy laws and ethical principles. MCA graduates must refuse such requests and explain the legal risks, including potential penalties under the IT Act or GDPR. Ethical IT professionals prioritize user rights and advocate for legitimate alternatives like transparency in monitoring tools that comply with privacy regulations.

18. Analyze the ethical challenges of using AI-based lie detection systems in recruitment processes.
Answer: AI lie detection in recruitment may be inaccurate and discriminate against certain groups due to biased algorithms. MCA graduates developing such tools must ensure fairness, transparency, and allow human oversight in decisions. Ethical practices involve testing systems for bias, explaining their limitations, and adhering to labor laws to protect candidates' rights.

19. Explain how IT professionals can ethically address data retention policies for e-commerce platforms.
Answer: Data retention policies dictate how long user data is stored. Storing data indefinitely increases privacy risks and may violate laws like GDPR. MCA graduates should implement policies that limit data retention to only what is necessary for operations, secure stored data, and provide users with options to delete their accounts and data. Ethical practices build trust and ensure legal compliance.

20. Discuss the legal and ethical responsibilities of IT professionals in securing medical IoT devices.
Answer: Medical IoT devices collect sensitive health data, making them a target for cyberattacks. Laws like HIPAA mandate strict data protection measures. MCA graduates developing such devices must use encryption, ensure secure updates, and design systems resilient to breaches. Ethical considerations include prioritizing patient safety and preventing unauthorized access to life-critical devices.

21. Evaluate how IT professionals should handle ethical concerns in facial recognition for law enforcement.
Answer: Facial recognition assists in crime prevention but may lead to wrongful arrests and privacy infringements. MCA graduates must ensure transparency, eliminate biases in training data, and advocate for oversight mechanisms. Ethical use requires limiting deployment to lawful purposes and ensuring compliance with privacy laws to avoid misuse.

22. Discuss the role of IT professionals in ensuring accessibility compliance in mobile applications.
Answer: Accessibility laws mandate apps cater to users with disabilities. MCA graduates should design with inclusivity in mind, implementing features like screen reader compatibility and high-contrast modes. Ethical practices ensure everyone can use apps regardless of physical limitations while meeting legal obligations under frameworks like WCAG and the Rights of Persons with Disabilities Act.

23. Analyze the ethical challenges of developing persuasive technologies for children.
Answer: Persuasive technologies may encourage addictive behavior in children. MCA graduates must avoid manipulative design, comply with laws like COPPA, and provide parental controls. Ethical design promotes education and healthy use while safeguarding children's privacy and mental well-being.

24. Explain how IT professionals should ethically manage data collection for smart city projects.
Answer: Smart cities collect massive data for efficient services but raise privacy concerns. MCA graduates should ensure informed consent, anonymize data, and limit collection to necessary purposes. Ethical management involves complying with privacy laws and balancing innovation with citizen rights to avoid creating surveillance-heavy environments.

25. Discuss the legal implications of a data breach in a multinational corporation.
Answer: Multinational corporations must comply with privacy laws in each jurisdiction. A data breach may trigger reporting requirements under laws like GDPR or India's PDP Bill and lead to hefty penalties. MCA graduates must develop global incident response strategies, encrypt sensitive data, and ensure cross-border compliance to minimize legal repercussions.

26. Evaluate how IT professionals can ethically handle requests for user data from government agencies.
Answer: Government data requests must comply with privacy laws and due process. MCA graduates should verify the legality of requests, disclose only necessary information, and inform users where possible. Ethical handling ensures compliance with laws like GDPR and avoids misuse of user data.

27. Discuss how IT professionals can prevent misuse of deepfake technologies.
Answer: Deepfakes can harm reputations and spread misinformation. MCA graduates should develop detection tools, educate users, and implement watermarks in media creation platforms. Ethical practices align with cyber laws that criminalize malicious use of deepfakes and protect individuals from digital harm.

28. Explain how IT professionals should manage privacy concerns in wearable health devices.
Answer: Wearables collect sensitive health metrics, making data security critical. MCA graduates must implement encryption, minimize data sharing, and comply with laws like HIPAA. Ethical practices include clear privacy policies, user consent, and options to disable tracking features, protecting users' autonomy.

29. Discuss the ethical considerations of creating algorithmic content moderation systems.
Answer: Algorithmic moderation helps filter harmful content but may suppress free speech or exhibit bias. MCA graduates should design systems with human oversight, fairness audits, and appeal mechanisms. Ethical moderation balances user safety with freedom of expression, aligning with platform liability under cyber laws.

30. Analyze the legal challenges in prosecuting cybercrimes across international borders.
Answer: Jurisdictional issues, differing laws, and lack of cooperation make cross-border cybercrime prosecution difficult. MCA graduates working on international platforms must design systems compliant with global standards and assist in lawful data sharing to support investigations.

31. Explain how IT professionals can ensure ethical practices in data analytics for targeted advertising.
Answer: Targeted ads rely on analyzing user behavior, raising privacy concerns. MCA graduates must ensure anonymization, provide opt-out options, and avoid manipulative tactics. Ethical advertising aligns with data protection laws and promotes transparency with users.

32. Discuss the ethical challenges in designing AI-based hiring systems for global organizations.
Answer: Global hiring systems must account for cultural and legal differences while avoiding algorithmic bias. MCA graduates should ensure diverse datasets, explainable AI models, and compliance with anti-discrimination laws. Ethical systems promote fairness and inclusivity in recruitment.

33. Evaluate how IT professionals can ethically design blockchain systems for voting applications.
Answer: Blockchain voting enhances transparency but may exclude non-tech-savvy citizens. MCA graduates should design user-friendly systems, secure anonymity, and comply with election laws. Ethical design promotes accessibility and prevents manipulation of democratic processes.

34. Explain how IT professionals can ethically manage user consent in social networking apps.
Answer: Social apps often collect extensive personal data. MCA graduates should design clear consent forms, allow users to control data sharing, and comply with privacy laws like GDPR. Ethical consent management builds trust and prevents misuse of sensitive information.

35. Discuss the role of IT professionals in preventing cyberbullying on digital platforms.
Answer: Cyberbullying harms victims emotionally and is punishable under cyber laws. MCA graduates can integrate content filters, reporting tools, and awareness programs to help platforms detect and address such behaviors ethically and legally.

36. Analyze how IT professionals should handle insider threats ethically in organizations.
Answer: Insider threats involve employees misusing access to harm systems. MCA graduates should design robust access controls, monitor for unusual activity, and educate staff on security policies. Ethical practices respect employee privacy while protecting organizational assets in compliance with laws.

37. Explain the ethical and legal considerations in developing AI-based health diagnosis systems.
Answer: AI diagnosis tools must avoid biases and errors that could endanger patients. MCA graduates should work with medical professionals, ensure data privacy, and comply with health regulations like HIPAA. Ethical AI complements doctors and safeguards user trust.

38. Discuss the ethical implications of designing persuasive financial applications.
Answer: Financial apps that nudge user behavior risk encouraging overspending or risky investments. MCA graduates must design transparent systems that prioritize user financial health and comply with regulations on responsible advertising.

39. Evaluate how IT professionals can ethically handle the design of workplace surveillance tools.
Answer: Workplace surveillance may boost productivity but risks privacy violations. MCA graduates should ensure transparency, collect only necessary data, and comply with labor laws to balance organizational goals with employee rights.

40. Explain the legal frameworks governing cryptocurrency transactions.
Answer: Cryptocurrencies face varying regulations worldwide. Some countries ban them, while others impose strict anti-money laundering (AML) rules. MCA graduates must design systems that comply with evolving crypto laws to prevent legal risks for users and platforms.

41. Discuss the ethical challenges of creating immersive virtual reality platforms.
Answer: VR platforms can impact mental health, privacy, and inclusivity. MCA graduates should design with age-appropriate safeguards, clear user policies, and prevent exploitation or addictive behaviors.

42. Analyze how IT professionals can ensure compliance with accessibility standards in government portals.
Answer: Government portals must be accessible to users with disabilities under laws like the Rights of Persons with Disabilities Act. MCA graduates should implement WCAG standards and test usability across diverse user groups for compliance.

43. Explain the role of IT professionals in securing cloud computing environments ethically.
Answer: Cloud security involves protecting user data from breaches and unauthorized access. MCA graduates should design systems with encryption, secure APIs, and compliance with privacy laws to build trust in cloud platforms.

44. Discuss the legal challenges of tackling online piracy in streaming services.
Answer: Streaming platforms face piracy through illegal downloads and unauthorized distribution. MCA graduates can implement watermarking, secure DRM systems, and cooperate with authorities to enforce copyright laws.

45. Evaluate the ethical responsibilities of IT professionals in preventing misinformation on social media.
Answer: Misinformation spreads rapidly on social platforms, impacting public opinion and safety. MCA graduates should design systems to flag false content, collaborate with fact-checkers, and balance moderation with free speech laws.

46. Explain how cyber laws regulate digital wallets and online payment systems.
Answer: Digital wallets are governed by financial regulations ensuring secure transactions and user protection. MCA graduates working on these systems must integrate encryption, fraud detection tools, and comply with RBI or global fintech laws.

47. Discuss the role of IT professionals in promoting digital literacy for cybersecurity.
Answer: Digital literacy helps users recognize cyber threats and practice safe online behavior. MCA graduates can design awareness campaigns and user-friendly tools to complement legal efforts in reducing cybercrime.

48. Analyze how IT professionals should ethically manage algorithmic transparency in financial platforms.
Answer: Transparency in financial algorithms builds trust and prevents unfair practices. MCA graduates should design explainable systems, allow user insights, and comply with financial regulations on fairness and accountability.

49. Explain the ethical considerations of using AI chatbots in mental health services.
Answer: AI chatbots provide support but lack human empathy and risk data breaches. MCA graduates must ensure privacy, inform users of limitations, and involve professionals in designing ethically responsible tools.

50. Discuss how IT professionals can prevent data misuse in educational platforms.
Answer: Educational platforms store sensitive student data, requiring secure storage and access controls. MCA graduates should design systems that comply with child data protection laws and prevent unauthorized sharing or exploitation of student information.

51. Explain how IT professionals should address ethical concerns in designing child-friendly online platforms.
Answer: Child-friendly online platforms require strict compliance with privacy and safety standards. Laws like COPPA (Children's Online Privacy Protection Act) and India's IT Rules mandate obtaining parental consent before data collection. MCA graduates must design systems that protect children from harmful content, avoid manipulative advertising, and ensure age-appropriate interactions. Ethical practices include implementing robust parental controls and educating stakeholders on responsible design, ensuring platforms remain safe and legally compliant for minors.

52. Discuss how cyber laws regulate online misinformation during elections.
Answer: Misinformation during elections undermines democracy and is punishable under cyber laws like the IT Act and Representation of People Act in India. MCA graduates working on social media platforms must develop AI-driven fact-checking tools, enable content flagging, and work with election authorities to remove harmful content swiftly. Ethical practices include balancing free speech with the need to preserve electoral integrity and public trust.

53. Analyze the ethical and legal implications of AI-generated content in digital media.
Answer: AI-generated content raises concerns about intellectual property rights, misinformation, and accountability. Laws are evolving to address ownership and liability for AI creations. MCA graduates must ensure proper attribution, watermarking of AI outputs, and avoid creating deceptive content. Ethical considerations involve transparency with users about AI involvement and adherence to cyber laws to prevent misuse.

54. Explain how IT professionals should handle ethical dilemmas in reporting security vulnerabilities.
Answer: Reporting security vulnerabilities requires balancing user protection and organizational interests. MCA graduates should follow responsible disclosure practices by informing the affected organization first, allowing time for a fix before going public. Ethical practices avoid exploiting vulnerabilities for personal gain and comply with laws that protect ethical hackers acting in good faith.

55. Discuss the legal requirements for data breach notifications in financial institutions.
Answer: Financial institutions are legally required to notify regulators and affected customers about data breaches within specified timeframes, such as GDPR's 72-hour rule. MCA graduates must design systems with breach detection capabilities and establish incident response teams to meet legal obligations, minimize financial loss, and maintain trust.

56. Evaluate the ethical responsibilities of IT professionals in designing persuasive e-learning platforms.
Answer: E-learning platforms often use gamification to engage learners but risk promoting addictive behaviors. MCA graduates should design ethically by ensuring transparency in algorithms, offering healthy usage reminders, and protecting user data. Compliance with privacy laws safeguards sensitive educational information and promotes responsible technology use.

57. Explain how IT professionals can ensure ethical practices in virtual currencies and blockchain systems.
Answer: Virtual currencies present opportunities but also risks like fraud and money laundering. Laws like India's Cryptocurrency Bill propose strict compliance requirements. MCA graduates must integrate KYC (Know Your

Customer) protocols, anti-money laundering checks, and transparent transaction histories to ensure ethical blockchain use and compliance with evolving regulations.

58. Discuss how cyber laws address identity theft in social networking sites.
Answer: Identity theft on social platforms involves impersonation or misuse of personal data. Cyber laws criminalize such actions, empowering victims to seek redress. MCA graduates can design systems with strong verification processes, two-factor authentication, and reporting tools to prevent impersonation and align platforms with legal frameworks.

59. Analyze the legal and ethical considerations of cloud storage services for global users.
Answer: Cloud services storing data globally must comply with diverse privacy laws, such as GDPR and India's data localization policies. MCA graduates should design systems with encryption, localized storage options, and transparency in data handling. Ethical practices involve informing users about where and how their data is stored and ensuring secure cross-border transfers.

60. Explain how IT professionals can mitigate risks of cyber espionage in multinational organizations.
Answer: Cyber espionage targets trade secrets and critical infrastructure. MCA graduates must deploy advanced intrusion detection systems, encrypt sensitive communications, and comply with legal obligations to report espionage attempts. Ethical considerations include training employees on security protocols and balancing vigilance with respect for user privacy.

61. Discuss how cyber laws regulate fake news during health emergencies.
Answer: Fake news during health crises causes public panic and is penalized under cyber laws like India's IT Act. MCA graduates working on information platforms must design fact-checking systems, collaborate with health authorities, and moderate harmful content swiftly to comply with regulations and protect public safety.

62. Evaluate the ethical implications of AI-driven hiring tools in eliminating human bias.
Answer: AI hiring tools can reduce human bias but risk perpetuating algorithmic bias if trained on flawed datasets. MCA graduates should ensure fairness audits, diverse training data, and transparent decision-making processes. Ethical systems balance efficiency with inclusivity and comply with employment laws to ensure equitable hiring practices.

63. Explain how IT professionals can ethically manage user consent in IoT ecosystems.
Answer: IoT devices often collect continuous user data, requiring explicit and informed consent. MCA graduates should design systems with clear opt-in options, provide users with data control features, and comply with privacy laws like GDPR. Ethical consent management builds trust and protects user autonomy.

64. Discuss the legal challenges in tackling cyberbullying among teenagers.
Answer: Cyberbullying laws empower authorities to act against online harassment, but enforcement is challenging due to anonymity and cross-platform issues. MCA graduates can develop detection tools, reporting systems, and awareness programs on platforms to prevent and address cyberbullying while ensuring compliance with legal frameworks.

65. Analyze how IT professionals should address ethical concerns in automated stock trading systems.
Answer: Automated trading systems execute rapid decisions but may amplify market volatility or disadvantage smaller investors. MCA graduates should design systems with safeguards, transparency in algorithms, and compliance with financial regulations to prevent manipulation and promote ethical financial practices.

66. Explain the ethical responsibilities of IT professionals in handling whistleblower reports.
Answer: Whistleblower reports often involve sensitive organizational data. MCA graduates should ensure secure reporting systems, protect whistleblower identities, and act on concerns ethically. Compliance with whistleblower protection laws ensures organizational accountability and prevents retaliation.

67. Discuss how IT professionals can promote ethical use of AI in online advertising.
Answer: AI in advertising personalizes user experiences but risks manipulation and privacy invasion. MCA graduates should ensure transparency in ad targeting, provide opt-out options, and comply with data protection laws to maintain ethical and responsible practices.

68. Evaluate the legal frameworks governing the ethical use of drones for delivery services.
Answer: Drone delivery services must comply with aviation and privacy laws to prevent accidents and unauthorized surveillance. MCA graduates developing drone systems should include geofencing, secure communication protocols, and adhere to regulations like India's DGCA guidelines. Ethical deployment ensures safety and public trust.

69. Explain how cyber laws regulate access to sensitive data in educational institutions.
Answer: Educational institutions handle sensitive student data and must comply with privacy laws. MCA graduates should design secure systems, limit access to authorized personnel, and ensure encryption of sensitive records to meet legal and ethical standards.

70. Discuss the ethical challenges in designing metaverse platforms for diverse user groups.
Answer: Metaverse platforms must ensure inclusivity, prevent harassment, and protect user privacy. MCA graduates should implement content moderation, identity protection tools, and accessibility features. Ethical practices align with evolving cyber laws to create safe virtual environments.

71. Analyze how IT professionals can ethically design productivity monitoring tools for remote workers.
Answer: Productivity monitoring tools risk invading employee privacy if misused. MCA graduates should prioritize transparency, collect only work-related data, and comply with labor laws. Ethical tools balance organizational needs with respect for employees' rights and autonomy.

72. Explain how cyber laws regulate phishing attacks targeting financial institutions.
Answer: Phishing attacks targeting banks are criminal offenses under the IT Act. MCA graduates working on financial systems should implement anti-phishing mechanisms, multi-factor authentication, and user education programs to meet legal requirements and protect customers.

73. Discuss how IT professionals can ethically address algorithmic bias in credit scoring systems.
Answer: Credit scoring algorithms risk excluding certain demographics if biased. MCA graduates should ensure diverse datasets, perform fairness testing, and provide users with explanations for decisions. Ethical systems comply with financial regulations and promote equitable access to credit.

74. Evaluate the ethical implications of AI-powered virtual assistants in healthcare.
Answer: Virtual assistants improve healthcare delivery but may misinterpret patient needs or compromise sensitive data. MCA graduates must involve healthcare professionals in design, ensure robust data security, and inform users of limitations to promote ethical adoption.

75. Explain how IT professionals can promote cybersecurity awareness in rural areas.
Answer: Rural communities often lack digital literacy, making them vulnerable to cyber threats. MCA graduates can develop awareness programs in local languages, design user-friendly tools, and collaborate with governments to promote safe technology use while aligning with national cybersecurity policies.

76. Discuss the ethical implications of using AI to monitor student behavior in online learning platforms.
Answer: AI monitoring tools track student behavior to detect cheating or assess engagement, but they raise concerns about privacy, consent, and psychological impact. MCA graduates designing such systems must ensure transparency, inform students about data collection practices, and implement privacy safeguards. Ethical practices include limiting monitoring to academic purposes, providing opt-out options where feasible, and complying with data protection laws like GDPR to avoid misuse or discrimination.

77. Explain how cyber laws regulate cyber extortion and ransomware attacks.
Answer: Cyber extortion, including ransomware attacks, is illegal under laws like the IT Act in India. Organizations are advised not to pay ransoms as it encourages criminal activity. MCA graduates working in cybersecurity should design systems with regular backups, incident response plans, and encryption to prevent such attacks. Reporting breaches to authorities and collaborating with law enforcement ensures legal compliance and supports broader efforts to curb cyber extortion.

78. Evaluate the ethical responsibilities of IT professionals in developing emotion-detection technologies.
Answer: Emotion-detection technologies analyze user expressions or voice to infer feelings, but they risk privacy violations and misinterpretation. MCA graduates must design such tools responsibly by obtaining explicit consent, ensuring accuracy, and avoiding manipulative applications. Ethical use requires transparency, limited data retention, and adherence to laws regulating biometric data collection to safeguard user rights.

79. Discuss how IT professionals should ethically handle data collected by fitness tracking apps.
Answer: Fitness apps collect sensitive health and location data, raising privacy concerns. MCA graduates must ensure secure storage using encryption, obtain explicit user consent for data sharing, and comply with health data laws like HIPAA. Ethical practices involve transparency in data usage, allowing users to control sharing preferences, and avoiding selling data to third parties without consent.

80. Explain how cyber laws address online harassment and threats on professional networking sites.
Answer: Online harassment on professional networks violates cyber laws like the IT Act and IPC provisions in India. MCA graduates working on these platforms must design robust reporting tools, implement content moderation policies, and cooperate with authorities in investigating threats. Ethical practices promote safe professional interactions and support compliance with anti-harassment regulations.

81. Analyze how IT professionals can ensure data integrity in digital evidence for legal investigations.
Answer: Digital evidence integrity is crucial in legal proceedings to ensure admissibility in court. MCA graduates working in cybersecurity must implement secure logging systems, chain-of-custody protocols, and use forensic tools that preserve data authenticity. Ethical handling of evidence prevents tampering and aligns with cyber laws, supporting fair and transparent investigations.

82. Discuss the ethical challenges of using persuasive design in social media platforms.
Answer: Persuasive design in social media keeps users engaged but may promote addictive behaviors and harm mental health. MCA graduates must design responsibly by limiting exploitative features like endless scrolling and providing tools for managing screen time. Ethical practices prioritize user well-being while maintaining compliance with privacy and consumer protection laws.

83. Explain how IT professionals should manage legal and ethical concerns in cross-border cloud data storage.
Answer: Cross-border data storage raises challenges due to differing privacy laws like GDPR and India's proposed Data Protection Bill. MCA graduates must design systems with data localization options, encrypt data in transit and at rest, and ensure transparency about storage locations. Ethical practices include obtaining user consent and avoiding unauthorized access to sensitive data.

84. Evaluate how IT professionals can prevent algorithmic discrimination in financial loan approval systems.
Answer: Loan approval algorithms risk perpetuating biases against certain demographics. MCA graduates should conduct fairness audits, use diverse datasets, and provide explainable AI decisions. Ethical practices involve transparency, human oversight, and compliance with anti-discrimination laws to ensure equitable access to financial services.

85. Discuss how cyber laws regulate the sharing of sensitive government documents online.
Answer: Unauthorized sharing of government documents is a serious offense under the Official Secrets Act and the IT Act in India. MCA graduates working with sensitive systems must implement strict access controls, encryption,

and monitoring to prevent leaks. Ethical practices include reporting suspicious activities promptly and ensuring compliance with national security laws.

86. Explain the ethical considerations of designing AI chatbots for mental health support.
Answer: AI chatbots provide accessible mental health assistance but cannot replace human empathy or professional judgment. MCA graduates must design systems that maintain confidentiality, disclose limitations, and escalate critical cases to human counselors. Ethical practices ensure compliance with health data laws and prioritize user safety over automation.

87. Discuss how IT professionals should ethically address intellectual property disputes in software development.
Answer: Intellectual property disputes arise when code or designs are copied without authorization. MCA graduates must ensure they use licensed components, respect open-source licenses, and avoid plagiarism. Ethical practices involve proper attribution, contract clarity in collaborative projects, and compliance with copyright laws to prevent legal conflicts.

88. Analyze the legal challenges of regulating the dark web under international cyber laws.
Answer: The dark web facilitates anonymity, making it challenging to regulate illegal activities like trafficking or cybercrime. MCA graduates in cybersecurity can assist by developing tracking tools that respect privacy rights, cooperating with global law enforcement, and ensuring compliance with international frameworks like the Budapest Convention to combat cross-border cyber offenses.

89. Explain how cyber laws regulate the ethical use of CCTV surveillance in public places.
Answer: CCTV use is governed by privacy laws that require minimizing intrusion and ensuring data protection. MCA graduates must design systems with secure storage, restricted access, and clear signage informing citizens about surveillance. Ethical practices involve balancing security needs with individual privacy rights in compliance with legal frameworks.

90. Discuss the ethical implications of using location tracking in mobile advertising.
Answer: Location tracking enables targeted advertising but may infringe on user privacy. MCA graduates should ensure users are informed, obtain explicit consent, and provide opt-out mechanisms. Ethical practices align with privacy laws like GDPR and avoid manipulative or intrusive marketing tactics.

91. Evaluate how IT professionals can ethically manage algorithmic transparency in job recommendation platforms.
Answer: Job recommendation algorithms may unintentionally favor certain profiles. MCA graduates should design explainable AI systems, provide feedback mechanisms for users, and ensure fair opportunities. Ethical practices comply with anti-discrimination laws and foster trust among diverse user groups.

92. Explain how IT professionals can ensure ethical practices in AI-based autonomous vehicles.
Answer: Autonomous vehicles rely on AI to make split-second decisions, raising ethical concerns about responsibility in accidents. MCA graduates must design systems prioritizing safety, include human override options, and comply with road safety laws. Ethical practices involve transparent decision-making frameworks and collaboration with regulators.

93. Discuss how IT professionals can promote digital inclusion in rural cybersecurity initiatives.
Answer: Digital inclusion ensures rural populations benefit from cybersecurity measures. MCA graduates can develop user-friendly tools, translate resources into local languages, and conduct awareness campaigns to bridge the digital divide. Ethical practices align with government policies promoting equitable access to secure technologies.

94. Analyze the ethical responsibilities of IT professionals in managing e-waste from obsolete devices.
Answer: E-waste contains hazardous materials and raises environmental concerns. MCA graduates must promote sustainable designs, support recycling initiatives, and educate users about safe disposal. Ethical practices contribute to corporate social responsibility and align with environmental protection laws.

95. Explain how cyber laws regulate phishing scams targeting senior citizens.
Answer: Senior citizens are often targeted in phishing scams due to their lack of digital literacy. Cyber laws impose strict penalties for such offenses. MCA graduates designing systems for this demographic should include phishing detection, user education features, and easy reporting options to protect vulnerable users.

96. Discuss how IT professionals should ethically manage consent for health data sharing in research.
Answer: Health data sharing in research requires explicit consent and anonymization to protect participant privacy. MCA graduates must design systems that enable secure, controlled data sharing while complying with laws like HIPAA and GDPR. Ethical practices involve transparency and respecting participants' rights to withdraw consent.

97. Evaluate how IT professionals can ensure fairness in AI-powered credit card fraud detection systems.
Answer: AI fraud detection may flag legitimate transactions if not designed carefully. MCA graduates should balance security with user experience by incorporating human review processes and ensuring unbiased algorithms. Ethical practices comply with financial regulations while minimizing customer inconvenience.

98. Explain the ethical considerations of designing gamified workplace productivity tools.
Answer: Gamification motivates employees but can lead to unhealthy competition and stress. MCA graduates should design systems that promote collaboration, provide opt-out options, and respect user privacy. Ethical gamification balances engagement with employee well-being and legal labor standards.

99. Discuss how IT professionals should handle requests to bypass encryption in messaging apps.
Answer: Governments may request backdoors in encrypted apps for security reasons, but this compromises user privacy and security. MCA graduates must balance compliance with laws and ethical obligations to protect users. Transparent policies and legal review of such requests are essential to avoid misuse.

100. Explain how cyber laws regulate data portability in online platforms.
Answer: Data portability gives users the right to transfer their data between platforms. Laws like GDPR mandate secure export mechanisms. MCA graduates should design systems enabling easy, secure data transfer while ensuring compliance and maintaining user trust in digital ecosystems.

101. Discuss the ethical challenges in developing AI-powered decision-making tools for judicial systems.
Answer: AI tools in judicial systems can assist judges in evaluating cases but may perpetuate biases if algorithms are trained on skewed datasets. MCA graduates must ensure fairness, transparency, and human oversight in such tools. Ethical considerations include explaining AI recommendations clearly, safeguarding defendants' rights, and complying with privacy laws. Responsible AI design ensures technology supports rather than replaces human judgment in legal processes.

102. Explain how IT professionals should handle ethical concerns while building location-tracking apps for emergencies.
Answer: Location-tracking apps used in emergencies, like disaster response, require careful handling of user privacy. MCA graduates must obtain informed consent, limit data collection to crisis situations, and ensure secure storage. Ethical practices involve transparency about data usage and preventing misuse post-emergency, complying with laws such as GDPR to balance public safety and individual rights.

103. Evaluate the legal implications of copyright infringement in digital content creation platforms.
Answer: Copyright infringement occurs when users share protected material without authorization. Cyber laws, such as the Copyright Act and IT Act, impose fines and penalties for such actions. MCA graduates developing platforms must implement copyright detection tools, enforce takedown policies, and educate users on fair use to ensure compliance and protect creators' rights.

104. Discuss the role of IT professionals in implementing cybersecurity for critical infrastructure.
Answer: Critical infrastructure such as power grids and hospitals requires robust cybersecurity measures to prevent catastrophic disruptions. MCA graduates must design systems with intrusion detection, encrypted communications,

and redundancy to ensure resilience. Ethical practices involve complying with national security laws and regularly auditing systems to adapt to evolving threats.

105. Explain the ethical and legal considerations in designing smart home devices.
Answer: Smart home devices often collect audio, video, and usage patterns, creating privacy risks. MCA graduates should ensure explicit consent, provide data control options, and comply with data protection laws like GDPR. Ethical practices involve designing secure systems resistant to hacking and being transparent about data sharing with third parties.

106. Analyze how IT professionals should ethically handle user data in AI-driven marketing platforms.
Answer: AI marketing platforms analyze user behavior to personalize ads, but they risk overstepping privacy boundaries. MCA graduates must ensure data anonymization, allow users to opt out, and avoid manipulative targeting. Ethical systems comply with data protection laws, promote transparency, and respect user autonomy in the digital advertising space.

107. Discuss how cyber laws regulate illegal cryptocurrency mining activities.
Answer: Illegal cryptocurrency mining exploits systems without consent, consuming energy and degrading hardware. Cyber laws penalize unauthorized resource use and mandate compliance with energy and taxation regulations. MCA graduates working on security solutions must design detection tools to prevent cryptojacking and protect organizational systems from such misuse.

108. Explain how IT professionals can ethically design health data sharing systems for medical research.
Answer: Health data sharing enhances research but must prioritize patient privacy. MCA graduates should implement anonymization techniques, obtain informed consent, and comply with laws like HIPAA or India's PDP Bill. Ethical practices involve transparency about how data will be used and ensuring participants can opt out at any stage.

109. Evaluate how IT professionals can prevent exploitation of digital payment systems.
Answer: Digital payment systems face risks like phishing, fraud, and unauthorized transactions. MCA graduates must design multi-factor authentication, encryption, and fraud detection tools. Ethical practices include educating users about safe practices and complying with financial regulations to secure transactions.

110. Discuss how IT professionals can ethically address surveillance concerns in autonomous vehicles.
Answer: Autonomous vehicles collect location and behavioral data, raising surveillance concerns. MCA graduates should ensure data minimization, encryption, and user control over sharing. Ethical practices include transparent privacy policies and compliance with regulations to prevent misuse of sensitive travel patterns.

111. Explain the ethical considerations in deploying AI-powered content recommendation engines.
Answer: Recommendation engines can reinforce echo chambers and addictive behaviors. MCA graduates should design algorithms promoting diversity in content, provide users with customization options, and avoid exploiting vulnerabilities for engagement. Ethical systems balance personalization with user well-being and comply with platform liability laws.

112. Discuss how IT professionals should manage data portability in social networking platforms ethically.
Answer: Data portability allows users to move their information between platforms, as mandated by laws like GDPR. MCA graduates should design secure export and import tools, ensure data integrity, and prevent vendor lock-in. Ethical practices empower users while safeguarding against data leaks during transfers.

113. Evaluate the ethical challenges in AI-driven fraud detection for insurance claims.
Answer: AI in insurance fraud detection may incorrectly flag legitimate claims, causing delays or denials. MCA graduates should ensure explainable AI models, allow human review, and test algorithms for fairness. Ethical systems balance fraud prevention with protecting honest customers' rights.

114. Explain how IT professionals can ethically manage algorithmic pricing systems in e-commerce.
Answer: Algorithmic pricing adjusts prices dynamically but may lead to unfair practices like price discrimination. MCA graduates must design transparent pricing models, avoid exploiting user data, and comply with consumer protection laws. Ethical systems promote fairness and prevent anti-competitive behaviors in online marketplaces.

115. Discuss the role of IT professionals in ensuring ethical use of biometric time-tracking systems.
Answer: Biometric systems enhance security but raise privacy concerns. MCA graduates should ensure secure storage, provide alternative options for employees uncomfortable with biometrics, and comply with privacy laws. Ethical practices include limiting data usage strictly to time-tracking purposes and ensuring transparency.

116. Analyze how cyber laws address online financial fraud in international transactions.
Answer: International financial fraud involves phishing, fake websites, and unauthorized access to accounts. Cyber laws like the IT Act and global frameworks such as FATF promote cooperation between countries. MCA graduates must integrate secure payment gateways, encryption, and fraud monitoring tools to protect users and ensure cross-border compliance.

117. Discuss how IT professionals can ethically design algorithms for smart city surveillance.
Answer: Smart city surveillance enhances security but risks violating privacy. MCA graduates must design systems with anonymization, secure data access controls, and public transparency about monitoring practices. Ethical considerations involve balancing public safety with individual freedoms and complying with data protection laws.

118. Explain how IT professionals should handle requests for user data from law enforcement ethically.
Answer: Law enforcement data requests must align with privacy laws and due process. MCA graduates should verify the legality of requests, provide only necessary data, and inform users if laws permit. Ethical practices prevent unauthorized access and misuse while supporting legitimate investigations.

119. Evaluate the legal implications of hacking smart medical devices.
Answer: Hacking medical devices endangers lives and is a serious offense under cyber laws like the IT Act and health data regulations. MCA graduates designing such devices must integrate strong encryption, secure firmware updates, and regular vulnerability testing to prevent such attacks.

120. Discuss the ethical and legal responsibilities of IT professionals in protecting user anonymity on the internet.
Answer: Protecting anonymity is crucial for whistleblowers, activists, and vulnerable users. MCA graduates must design systems with encryption, avoid unnecessary tracking, and comply with privacy laws. Ethical practices respect user rights while balancing obligations to report illegal activities where required.

121. Explain how IT professionals can ensure compliance with accessibility laws in developing e-governance systems.
Answer: E-governance platforms must serve all citizens, including those with disabilities. MCA graduates should implement accessibility features like screen readers and keyboard navigation, ensuring compliance with laws like India's Rights of Persons with Disabilities Act and WCAG standards.

122. Discuss how IT professionals can ethically manage big data analytics in healthcare.
Answer: Big data analytics offers insights for healthcare but risks privacy breaches. MCA graduates should use anonymized datasets, comply with health data laws, and ensure ethical use to avoid discrimination or misuse of sensitive information.

123. Analyze the ethical challenges of using AI in workplace performance evaluations.
Answer: AI-based evaluations risk bias and lack transparency. MCA graduates must ensure fairness, allow employees to challenge AI decisions, and comply with labor laws. Ethical practices promote balanced assessments and maintain employee trust.

124. Explain how cyber laws regulate data breaches in educational institutions.
Answer: Educational institutions must protect sensitive student data under privacy laws like GDPR and India's PDP Bill. MCA graduates should design secure systems, establish breach notification protocols, and ensure legal compliance to protect students' rights.

125. Discuss the role of IT professionals in ensuring ethical innovation for emerging technologies.
Answer: Emerging technologies like AI, IoT, and blockchain bring new risks alongside benefits. MCA graduates should adopt privacy-by-design principles, anticipate societal impacts, and align innovations with ethical frameworks and legal standards to ensure responsible progress in the digital age.

126. Discuss the ethical implications of AI-powered predictive systems in monitoring employee productivity.
Answer: AI-based productivity monitoring tools can enhance organizational efficiency but risk invading employee privacy. MCA graduates must design systems that focus on work-related metrics, avoid collecting personal information, and ensure transparency with employees about monitoring practices. Ethical practices include providing opt-out options where feasible and adhering to labor laws that safeguard worker rights and prevent misuse of collected data.

127. Explain how IT professionals can ethically manage cybersecurity for online voting systems.
Answer: Online voting systems require robust security to maintain electoral integrity. MCA graduates must implement end-to-end encryption, multi-factor authentication, and regular vulnerability assessments. Ethical practices involve ensuring accessibility for all citizens, protecting voter anonymity, and complying with legal frameworks to prevent fraud and maintain public trust in digital democracy initiatives.

128. Evaluate the legal challenges of implementing cyber laws in decentralized blockchain applications.
Answer: Decentralized blockchain applications often lack a central authority, complicating legal enforcement. MCA graduates must ensure compliance with existing financial, privacy, and anti-money laundering regulations when designing such systems. Ethical practices include educating users about the limitations and legal risks of decentralized platforms and ensuring secure smart contract development.

129. Discuss the role of IT professionals in preventing cybercrime targeting elderly users.
Answer: Elderly users are often targeted through phishing scams, malware, and fraud due to limited digital literacy. MCA graduates can design user-friendly systems with simplified interfaces, integrate fraud detection tools, and conduct awareness campaigns. Ethical responsibilities involve ensuring accessibility and providing tools that empower seniors to navigate technology safely and securely.

130. Explain the ethical considerations of deploying biometric surveillance in public transportation systems.
Answer: Biometric surveillance in public transport improves safety but may violate citizens' privacy rights. MCA graduates must design systems that limit data collection, secure storage, and provide transparency about usage. Ethical practices involve anonymizing data wherever possible and complying with privacy laws to balance security needs and personal freedoms.

131. Analyze the ethical responsibilities of IT professionals in developing AI tools for law enforcement.
Answer: AI tools assist law enforcement in predicting crime patterns and identifying suspects, but they may perpetuate biases and infringe on civil liberties. MCA graduates should ensure fairness, include oversight mechanisms, and avoid misuse of AI for mass surveillance. Ethical practices align with legal standards and prioritize protecting fundamental human rights.

132. Discuss how cyber laws regulate the ethical use of drones for environmental monitoring.
Answer: Drones used for environmental monitoring must comply with aviation regulations and privacy laws. MCA graduates developing such systems should ensure secure data handling, avoid surveillance of private properties without consent, and adhere to guidelines like India's DGCA policies. Ethical deployment supports conservation efforts while respecting individual rights.

133. Explain how IT professionals can design ethical algorithms for financial trading platforms.
Answer: Algorithmic trading can lead to market manipulation or unfair advantages. MCA graduates should design systems with built-in safeguards against excessive volatility, ensure transparency in algorithmic decisions, and comply with financial regulations. Ethical practices involve protecting small investors and avoiding designs that exploit market loopholes.

134. Evaluate how IT professionals can prevent data misuse in AI-powered virtual assistants.
Answer: Virtual assistants process sensitive user data like conversations and preferences, posing privacy risks. MCA graduates must design systems that encrypt communications, limit data retention, and provide users with control over stored information. Ethical practices include disclosing data usage policies and ensuring compliance with global privacy laws like GDPR.

135. Discuss the ethical challenges of designing online platforms for whistleblower protection.
Answer: Whistleblower platforms require strong security to protect anonymity and prevent retaliation. MCA graduates should implement encryption, secure submission channels, and adhere to whistleblower protection laws. Ethical responsibilities include ensuring only authorized personnel access sensitive reports and fostering organizational accountability.

136. Explain how cyber laws regulate digital forensics in cybercrime investigations.
Answer: Digital forensics involves collecting electronic evidence for legal proceedings. Cyber laws require adherence to procedures that preserve data integrity and chain of custody. MCA graduates working in this domain must use certified forensic tools, maintain transparency, and ensure compliance with privacy rights while assisting in investigations.

137. Discuss how IT professionals should ethically handle AI-driven systems in predicting student success in educational platforms.
Answer: Predictive analytics in education can help identify students needing support but may unfairly label individuals based on incomplete data. MCA graduates should design systems that allow for human intervention, ensure algorithmic fairness, and comply with data privacy laws. Ethical practices avoid reinforcing stereotypes and provide constructive insights for educators.

138. Evaluate the legal implications of storing sensitive user data on public cloud servers.
Answer: Public cloud servers may store data across borders, raising compliance challenges with privacy laws like GDPR and India's PDP Bill. MCA graduates must design systems that encrypt data, provide localization options, and ensure cloud providers meet regulatory standards. Ethical practices involve informing users about storage locations and mitigating risks of unauthorized access.

139. Explain the ethical and legal challenges in designing AI tools for creditworthiness assessments.
Answer: AI tools for credit scoring risk perpetuating biases if trained on flawed historical data. MCA graduates must ensure fairness testing, transparent decision-making processes, and compliance with financial regulations. Ethical systems provide users with recourse to appeal AI decisions and avoid excluding vulnerable groups from access to credit.

140. Discuss how IT professionals can ethically manage cybersecurity in telemedicine platforms.
Answer: Telemedicine platforms handle sensitive health data, requiring robust security measures. MCA graduates should implement end-to-end encryption, secure user authentication, and comply with health data regulations like HIPAA. Ethical practices involve designing systems that protect patient confidentiality and prevent unauthorized access during consultations.

141. Analyze the ethical responsibilities of IT professionals in designing autonomous weapon systems.
Answer: Autonomous weapons raise ethical concerns about accountability, proportionality, and civilian harm. MCA graduates working on such systems should advocate for strict human oversight, avoid developing fully autonomous lethal systems, and comply with international humanitarian laws to prevent misuse in warfare.

142. Explain how cyber laws regulate online marketplaces to protect consumer rights.
Answer: Cyber laws require online marketplaces to provide secure transactions, protect user data, and resolve grievances promptly. MCA graduates should design platforms with secure payment systems, fraud detection tools, and clear return policies to comply with regulations like India's Consumer Protection (E-Commerce) Rules.

143. Discuss the ethical considerations in designing AI systems for workplace hiring and promotions.
Answer: AI systems in hiring can unintentionally discriminate against certain groups. MCA graduates should ensure diverse datasets, audit for bias regularly, and allow human oversight in decisions. Ethical practices include transparency in selection criteria and compliance with anti-discrimination laws to ensure fairness.

144. Evaluate how IT professionals can manage cybersecurity for critical financial systems ethically.
Answer: Financial systems are prime targets for cyberattacks, and breaches can have severe consequences. MCA graduates should implement multi-layered defenses, conduct regular security audits, and comply with financial cybersecurity frameworks. Ethical practices involve maintaining customer trust and protecting the stability of the financial ecosystem.

145. Explain how IT professionals can promote ethical innovation in emerging technologies like quantum computing.
Answer: Quantum computing promises immense power but poses risks like breaking current encryption standards. MCA graduates should advocate for ethical research, develop quantum-safe encryption methods, and collaborate with policymakers to ensure responsible deployment. Ethical innovation aligns with global security and legal frameworks to prevent misuse of advanced technologies.

9 789369 728

Printed at Repro India Ltd.